Take &Read

The Gospel of Matthew

Henry Wansbrough,
Edited by Adrian Graffy

Published in 2009 by Alive Publishing Ltd.
Graphic House, 124 City Road, Stoke on Trent, ST4 2PH.
Tel: +44 (0) 1782 745600.   Fax: +44 (0) 1782 745500
www.alivepublishing.co.uk

©2009 Alive Publishing
British Library Catalogue-in-Publication Data.
A catalogue record for this book is available from the British Library.

ISBN 978-1-906278-05-2

Contents

Foreword

One of the features of the Church of today is the rediscovery of the Bible. In the years since the Second Vatican Council this thirst for the Scriptures has become stronger and stronger. The desire for a deeper engagement with the Bible is clear from the enormous popularity of publications such as *Walk with Me* and *Bible Alive*.

Take and Read is designed to assist people in their need to understand the Bible more deeply. The series has been developed as a follow-up to the document 'The Gift of Scripture', which was produced in 2005 by the Bishops of England and Wales, and of Scotland, to mark the 40th anniversary of the Council document on Divine Revelation, *Dei Verbum*.

The story of the conversion of Saint Augustine to the Catholic faith inspired the title of the series. He recounts in his 'Confessions' how he heard a voice calling to him with the words *Tolle, lege* 'Take and Read'. At that moment he picked up the New Testament and read the first chapter his eyes fell upon, from the Letter to the Romans. His conversion was assured.

These books are a major new resource for prayerful reading of the Scriptures both for groups and for individuals. Passages from the Gospels are accompanied by commentary, quotations from the Fathers and from Church documents, Christian art and inspiring photographs, as well as suggestions for prayer and reflection.

It is a great pleasure to acknowledge the work of those who helped develop this series. Representatives from dioceses throughout Britain worked on the preparatory stages. Particular thanks should go to Anne White, Anne Dixon and Sister Vicky Hummell. I record my gratitude to the authors who have produced such rich commentary on the gospel passages. I am particularly pleased that Mike and Sue Conway of Alive Publishing agreed to publish the *Take and Read* series.

Take and Read will help you to delve more deeply into the Scriptures, to understand them better, and to pray with the Scriptures. *Take and Read* will assist you in *lectio divina*, that prayerful reading of Scripture which has always been central to the life of the Church.

Fr Adrian Graffy

And behold I heard a voice from a nearby house singing and frequently repeating, like a boy or a girl, I do not know which: Take and read; take and read. I grabbed the book and opened it and I read in silence the first chapter my eyes fell upon.

Augustine Confessions VIII, 29

I pray you, good Jesus,
that as you have graciously granted me to take
in with delight
the words that give knowledge of you,
so you will grant me in your kindness
to come at last to you, the source of all wisdom,
and to stand for ever before your face. Amen.

The Prayer of St Bede (to end a session)

Introduction to the Gospel of Matthew

The first gospel to be written was that of Mark. Most likely, a few years later, the young Christian Churches wanted a gospel which included more of the teachings of Jesus, for Mark concentrates on the personality of Jesus. They approached the Christian teacher whom we call Matthew, who edited Mark somewhat, and inserted five great collections of the teaching of Jesus. Most probably these teachings had been collected into a document known to both Matthew and Luke, but now lost, for large tracts of material are shared word for word by these two gospels. Matthew also added some of his own material, stories and details which he must have received by separate oral tradition, and which he was the first to write down.

It is clear from the interests and emphases of this gospel that Matthew and his community were Jews who had recognised Jesus as the Messiah of Judaism and so had become Christians. Matthew uses Jewish methods of argument, and is familiar with Jewish institutions. He stresses that Jesus fulfils the Jewish scriptures and especially the Jewish Law, though not in the way that his Jewish contemporaries favoured. This made for a decided tension between Matthew's community and their Jewish neighbours, amounting even to hostility and resulting in persecution of these Christian Jews. The same sort of tension is visible in the Gospel of John, and may well have been widespread towards the end of the first century.

Matthew also shows us a community which has settled down to live the Christian life. There is no longer the vivid expectation of an immediate Second Coming of Christ which we find in Mark. Matthew envisages a longer period of Christian living before the rewards and punishments of the final judgment. Meanwhile he is intensely conscious of the divine presence of Christ in the community of the Church, the new People of God, and of the authority which the Church exercises in Christ's name.

These twelve passages from the Gospel of Matthew have been selected to supplement the passages of Mark which were chosen to represent that gospel in that volume of *Take and Read*. They aim to show the specific teachings of Matthew and the interests of his Christian community. As with the selections from Mark, it will be valuable for you to read on your own the intervening passages of Matthew, which will help to give a rounded picture of the gospel and its teaching.

Opposite: The Magi and King Herod, from Bellver de Cerdanya, 14th century. Catalan art.

The Visit of the Wise Men

Hear the Word of God

Read Matthew 2:1-18

2¹ In the time of King Herod, after Jesus was born in Bethlehem of Judea, wise men from the East came to Jerusalem, ² asking, 'Where is the child who has been born king of the Jews? For we observed his star at its rising, and have come to pay him homage.' ³ When King Herod heard this, he was frightened, and all Jerusalem with him; ⁴ and calling together all the chief priests and scribes of the people, he inquired of them where the Messiah was to be born. ⁵ They told him, 'In Bethlehem of Judea; for so it has been written by the prophet: ⁶ 'And you, Bethlehem, in the land of Judah, are by no means least among the rulers of Judah; for from you shall come a ruler who is to shepherd my people Israel.''

⁷ Then Herod secretly called for the wise men and learned from them the exact time when the star had appeared. ⁸ Then he sent them to Bethlehem, saying, 'Go and search diligently for the child; and when you have found him, bring me word so that I may also go and pay him homage.' ⁹ When they had heard the king, they set out; and there, ahead of them, went the star that they had seen at its rising, until it stopped over the place where the child was. ¹⁰ When they saw that the star had stopped, they were overwhelmed with joy. ¹¹ On entering the house, they saw the child with Mary his mother; and they knelt down and paid him homage. Then, opening their treasure-chests, they offered him gifts of gold, frankincense, and myrrh. ¹² And having been warned in a dream not to return to Herod, they left for their own country by another road.

¹³ Now after they had left, an angel of the Lord appeared to Joseph in a dream and said, 'Get up, take the child and his mother, and flee to Egypt, and remain there until I tell you; for Herod is about to search for the child, to destroy him.' ¹⁴ Then Joseph got up, took the child and his mother by night, and went to Egypt, ¹⁵ and remained there until the death of Herod. This was to fulfil what had been spoken by the Lord through the prophet, 'Out of Egypt I have called my son.'

¹⁶ When Herod saw that he had been tricked by the wise men, he was infuriated, and he sent and killed all the children in and around Bethlehem who were two years old or under, according to the time that he had learned from the wise men. ¹⁷ Then was fulfilled what had been spoken through the prophet Jeremiah ¹⁸ 'A voice was heard in Ramah, wailing and loud lamentation, Rachel weeping for her children, she refused to be consoled, because they are no more.'

Understand the Word of God

This session will explore:

❖ Why Matthew adds stories about Jesus' infancy

❖ Why Matthew's gospel is full of scriptural quotations

❖ The contrast between King Herod and the Wise Men

❖ How Matthew views Jesus

Setting in the Gospel

The story of the visit of the Wise Men forms most of Matthew's second chapter. Mark's gospel, the first to be written, begins with the Baptism of Jesus. The reader could be left thinking that Jesus' special career began then, at his Baptism. So Matthew sets out to show that his special quality was already evident at his first appearance on earth. In the first chapter he shows how Jesus is the climax of all the promises and all the history of Judaism. By divine command (given through the angel in a dream) Joseph adopted him into the House of David, so that Jesus was a son of David, despite having no physical human father. Now in the second chapter Jesus is shown to be a second Moses, repeating in his own story the story of Moses. So by the time we get to the Baptism of Jesus, we know that Jesus is the fulfilment of all the Jewish hopes.

Altarpiece of the three wise men by
Hans Baldung Grien

What Kind of Text?

This type of writing is called in Hebrew 'midrash', a word which means 'searching'. It is searching out the meaning and fulness of a scriptural text, a sort of meditation on scripture, much used in Jewish writings at the time of Jesus. In this case, the author re-tells the story of Jesus in such a way that a reader familiar with the story of Moses will be struck by the similarity of their two stories. The similarity with the slightly elaborated version of the story of Moses popular at the time is even greater. It looks as though Matthew was familiar with this version. It includes, for instance, the notice that the whole city was thrown into confusion by the news that Moses had been born (compare verse 3 of our text).

Jesus goes through the same process as Moses did: the ruler hears that a rival has been born and tries unsuccessfully to kill the child. Before long the new leader has to flee into exile (as Moses fled into Midian in *Exodus* 2:15), and remains there until an angel appears with the message that it is safe to return. The angel who tips Joseph the wink to return uses almost exactly the same words as the divine message to Moses in Exodus 4:19.

Exodus 4:19-20 reads:

The Lord said to Moses in Midian, 'Go back to Egypt, for all those who were seeking your life are dead.' So Moses took his wife and his sons, put them on a donkey, and went back to the land of Egypt.

The full story of Moses' childhood is told in Exodus 1-2.

Flight into Egypt, Virgin Mary with baby Jesus, and Joseph, Predella panel from Gentile da Fabriano.

- 12 -

Like all the other incidents in the stories of Jesus' infancy in chapters 1-2, Matthew concludes this section by pointing out that it fulfils the scriptures. These applications may seem a little forced to us, but they closely follow the way scripture is used in contemporary Jewish writings.

Massacre of the Innocents, 1565 by Pieter the Elder Bruegel, (1528-1569).

Does this mean that the story is made up? Not at all! Herod was perfectly capable of behaving like this. There would not be many male babies in a tiny hill-village like Bethlehem. Herod killed several of his sons and close relations on suspicion that they were trying to supplant him. The emperor Augustus (who knew him well) punned that he would rather be Herod's pig than his son (hys=pig hyios=son in Greek). Herod didn't eat pork! As Herod was dying he ordered that all the notables of the country should be killed, to ensure that there was real mourning in the land. The order was not carried out.

Commentary: verse by verse reading

The Visit of the Magi

The Book of Job reads:

'Now when Job's three friends heard of all these troubles that had come upon him, each of them set out from his home – Eliphaz the Temanite, Bildad the Shuhite and Zophar the Naamathite. They met together to go and console and comfort him. When they saw him from a distance they did not recognize him, and they raised their voices and wept aloud; they tore their robes and threw dust on their heads.'

(Job 2:11-12)

The Cathedral at Cologne in Germany is dedicated to the Three Kings, whose traditional names are Caspar, Melchior and Balthasar. Their relics are held to be within the Cathedral.

From a sermon of St Basil the Great:

The stars traverse the skies; the wise men journey from gentile lands, while the earth receives its Redeemer in the cave. There must be no one without some gift to offer, no one unmindful of the gratitude we owe. Let us celebrate the world's salvation, the day Christ was born in our humanity, for today Adam's sentence is reversed.
(PL 31,1471)

Isaiah 40:3 reads:

A voice cries out: 'In the wilderness prepare the way of the Lord, make straight in the desert a highway for our God.'

v.1 King Herod the Great was a colourful character who deserved the name 'Great'. He ruled Palestine autocratically for 36 years, dying in 4 BC. With his immense wealth he built not only the Temple in Jerusalem, one of the wonders of the ancient world, but a series of palaces, the ruins of which still survive to this day in Palestine. He also gave generously to the cities around the Mediterranean where Jews formed an important part of the population. But he would brook no rivals!

The wise men (they are not 'kings', and the number 'three' is only a guess, founded on their three kinds of gift) come from the East, the traditional land of wisdom and mystery. The wise counsellors who attempted to comfort Job in his suffering came from there too.

v.2 The wisdom of the stars is particularly associated with the East. Much of our knowledge of astronomy stems ultimately from Babylon, as do the lunar month of 28 days, and the division of the hour and the minute into units of 60. However, the appearance of a star at the birth of a 'star' (not merely football-stars and rock-stars) is reported at the birth of many great men in antiquity, such as Nimrod or Alexander the Great. One commentator even says, 'It was inconceivable that a great man could be born without a star being seen.' In the Bible this star is also the fulfilment of Balaam's prophecy in Numbers 24:17: 'I see him, but not now; I behold him, but not near – a star shall come out of Jacob, and a sceptre shall rise out of Israel.' There is no point in trying to relate such reports to actual astral phenomena.

vv.3-4 The expectation of a Messiah (a Hebrew term for which the Greek equivalent is 'Christ') was widespread at this time, and no doubt there were many theories about where he would appear. The authors of the Dead Sea Scrolls found at Qumran, relying on Isaiah 40:3, expected the Messiah to come from the desert, and went out to wait for him there.

With its Jewish connotations, the title Messiah was particularly important to Matthew, but Jesus himself was wary of it, since many people saw the Messiah as a political figure who would expel the Roman invaders. Jesus was wholly concentrated on the Kingship of his Father, not on his own titles. He saw this Sovereignty of God to consist in doing the will of the Father, in the welcome to sinners, in the removal of pain, sickness, suffering, fear and alienation.

vv.5-6 To Matthew it is important that these details of scripture should be fulfilled, and he concludes each section of the infancy stories with such a quotation. Bethlehem was the city of David, or rather the little shepherding village from which David, son of Jesse, came (1 *Samuel* 16:1). Jesus' birth at Bethlehem is one of the few facts of Jesus' infancy which is attested by both Matthew and Luke. However, this quotation about Bethlehem from the prophet Micah in fact turns it round. The original prophecy read, 'You, Bethlehem, the least of the clans of Judah'.

vv.7-10 Herod's nice irony in pretending that he wants to venerate the child is matched by Matthew's irony: the Jew, who should recognise the Messiah but wants to kill him, is contrasted with the gentile outsiders, who actually do venerate him. At the end of the gospel the same irony is seen in the contrast between the high priest Caiaphas, who unjustly condemns Jesus, and the gentile Pilate, who declares Jesus' innocence.

vv.11-12 The traditional symbolism of the gifts is gold for kingship, frankincense for priesthood and myrrh for suffering. It has also been suggested that frankincense and myrrh, both much used in spells, may mean that these eastern magicians (the Greek word *magoi* has that connotation) lay down or offer up to Jesus both their superstitious practices and the gold which is the profit from such practices. It may also symbolise more generally the fulfilment of such prophecies as Isaiah 60:1-5, that the wealth of the nations will be brought in homage to Jerusalem.

Bethlehem is a small town about 8 kilometres south of Jerusalem. It is mentioned in two more significant texts in the Hebrew Scriptures. It is the town where Ruth, from the land of Moab, who will be the great-grandmother of David, comes to settle with her mother-in-law Naomi (Ruth 1:22). It is the town to which the prophet Samuel travels in search of a new king, and where he eventually finds and anoints David, son of Jesse (1 Samuel 16:13). The full text from the prophet Micah reads:

But you, O Bethlehem of Ephrathah, who are one of the least of the clans of Judah, from you shall come forth for me one who is to rule in Israel, whose origin is from of old, from ancient days.

(Micah 5:1/5:2)

The magi represent the wisdom of this world. All this had to be laid at the feet of the child who is indeed the Word, but who also has yet to learn to shape his lips and tongue to his native language. The magi thus submit, consecrate, sacrifice the wisdom of the world to the folly of God's infancy, the folly of the cross. They plunge the illusory light of merely human brilliance into the darkness of the cave.

(From 'The Son's Course' by Gerald Vann OP, chapter 10)

The Flight into Egypt by Jesus Mafa.

This prophecy from the third part of the Book of Isaiah, addressed to the restored city of Jerusalem, reads as follows: 'Arise, shine, for your light has come, and the glory of the Lord has risen upon you. For darkness shall cover the earth, and thick darkness the peoples; but the Lord will arise upon you, and his glory will appear over you. Nations shall come to your light, and kings to the brightness of your dawn. Lift up your eyes and look around; they all gather together, they come to you; your sons shall come from far away, and your daughters shall be carried on their nurses' arms. Then you shall see and be radiant; your heart shall thrill and rejoice, because the abundance of the sea shall be brought to you, and the wealth of the nations shall come to you.' (*Isaiah* 60:1-5).

The Flight into Egypt

v.13 Apart from the angel who explains the empty tomb to the disciples, as in Matthew 28:6, angels appear in the gospels only in the infancy-stories. Angels and dreams occur frequently in contemporary Jewish literature as means of conveying divine messages, and in fact the Greek word *angelos* means 'messenger'. The flight into Egypt parallels the flight of Moses from Egypt into Midian in Exodus 2:15; the common factor is that both flee into exile from their homeland.

This is the last time in scripture that Joseph is named as taking part in the story. In Matthew he is amusingly incommunicative, never explaining his game-plan to Mary, just grabbing the two of them and taking them off! Medieval legend deduced from his non-appearance in Jesus' ministry that he had died before then. In medieval mystery-plays he is often cast as the comic-relief old man, but there is no basis for this in scripture.

v.15 Historical records show that Herod died in 4 BC. If the calculation was correct that Jesus was 'two years old or under', that would mean paradoxically that Jesus was born in or after 6 BC. The confusion comes from a mistake in the calculations of Dionysius Exiguus, the sixth-century monk who was responsible for working out the turn of the eras.

This section again is 'signed off' by a scriptural quotation fulfilled. This passage, Hosea 11:1-4, is one of the loveliest expressions in the Bible of God's fatherly (or motherly) love for the people Israel.

It reads as follows: 'When Israel was a child, I loved him, and out of Egypt I called my son. The more I called them, the more they went from me; they kept sacrificing to the Baals, and offering incense to idols. Yet it was I who taught Ephraim to walk, I took them up in my arms; but they did not know that I healed them. I led them with cords of human kindness, with bands of love. I was to them like those who lift infants to their cheeks. I bent down to them and fed them.' (*Hosea 11:1-4*)

The Preface for feasts of St Joseph says this about him:

He is that just man, that wise and loyal servant, whom you placed at the head of your family. With a husband's love he cherished Mary, the virgin Mother of God. With fatherly care he watched over Jesus Christ, your Son, who was conceived by the power of the Holy Spirit.

The Death of the Innocents

v.16 Herod's killing of the Holy Innocents need not have been the dramatic massacre sometimes depicted in art. Bethlehem at that time would have had few male children in a bracket of two years. Perhaps this makes the slaughter all the more horrific, though in any case it was well within Herod's pattern of behaviour. It also parallels the slaughter of the Hebrew children by Pharaoh narrated in the first chapter of the Book of Exodus. Exodus 1:22 reads: 'The Pharaoh commanded all his people, 'Every boy that is born to the Hebrews you shall throw into the Nile, but you shall let every girl live."

vv.17-18 These verses present another slightly forced fulfilment of scripture. The passage from the prophet Jeremiah originally referred to Rachel mourning for her children, the northern tribes of Israel, after they were exiled by the Assyrians. But a later tradition located Rachel's tomb at Bethlehem (where it is still venerated), and this enables Matthew to apply the passage to the death of the Holy Innocents. It is always important to Matthew to show that God's plan announced in scripture (in this case *Jeremiah* 31:15) comes to fruition in Jesus.

Though they knew it not, these children died for Christ, and their parents are mourning the deaths of Martyrs. How great was the grace thus bestowed! Not through merits of their own did those infants conquer the great adversary. They could not speak, yet they confessed Christ. Helpless to enter the battle, they still carried off the palm of victory.

(From a Sermon by St Quodvultdeus, PL 40, 655)

Opposite: The Massacre of the Innocents, from the 'Book of Hours of Louis d'Orleans', 1469.

The Word Lives On

The passage on the Visit of the Magi forms, of course, the gospel reading for the Feast of the Epiphany each year. The Flight into Egypt is read on the Feast of the Holy Family in Year A, a reminder of the closeness of the members of the holy family to one another in this frightening escape. The martyrdom of the Innocent Children is celebrated three days after Christmas, on 28th December. They are celebrated not because they died for their faith in Christ, but because they died in the place of Christ.

In the Eastern Church the Epiphany is still, as it formerly was also in the Western Church, a more important festival than Jesus' birthday. 'Epiphany' means 'appearance' or 'manifestation', and the centre of the festival was and is the acknowledgement of Jesus by the wise men, who represent the gentile nations. This is the day on which Jesus was made known to the world. A subsidiary part of the celebration, now transferred to the Feast of the Baptism of the Lord, was the manifestation of Jesus at the Jordan as the Lamb of God.

In the three magi let all the nations worship the author of the universe, and let God be known, not in Judaea alone but throughout the whole world.

(St Leo the Great, Sermon 3 on Epiphany)

The entrance to Nativity Church in Bethlehem.

Live the Word of God

Listen again to the reading: Matthew 2:1-18

What do you hear now?

Suggestions for reflection and prayer

Herod is the icon of the Chosen People failing to recognise the Messiah.

If Jesus came today, would he come first to you or to the less privileged members of society?

The Magi represent the nations who recognise the Messiah.

How aware are you of the diversity and richness of God's people?

Do I ever abuse my power to bully people less secure or less powerful than myself?

❖ Pray that you may use your talents and resources for the good of others, not merely for self-advancement.

Do I do enough to help the homeless and families in need?

❖ Pray that you may do what you can to create a more just and caring society.

Who was the last person in real need that you met? Did you help?

❖ Pray to recognise Christ in the poor and helpless.

In the magi, representatives of the neighbouring pagan religions, the Gospel sees the first-fruits of the nations, who welcome the good news of salvation through the Incarnation. The Epiphany shows that the full number of the nations now takes its place in the family of the patriarchs.

(Catechism of the Catholic Church n.528)

The Sermon on the Mount

Hear the Word of God

Read Matthew 5:1-20

5 [1] When Jesus saw the crowds, he went up the mountain; and after he sat down, his disciples came to him. [2] Then he began to speak, and taught them, saying:

[3] 'Blessed are the poor in spirit, for theirs is the kingdom of heaven.

[4] 'Blessed are those who mourn, for they will be comforted.

[5] 'Blessed are the meek, for they will inherit the earth.

[6] 'Blessed are those who hunger and thirst for righteousness, for they will be filled.

[7] 'Blessed are the merciful, for they will receive mercy.

[8] 'Blessed are the pure in heart, for they will see God.

[9] 'Blessed are the peacemakers, for they will be called children of God.

[10] 'Blessed are those who are persecuted for righteousness' sake, for theirs is the kingdom of heaven.

[11] 'Blessed are you when people revile you and persecute you and utter all kinds of evil against you falsely on my account. [12] Rejoice and be glad, for your reward is great in heaven, for in the same way they persecuted the prophets who were before you.

[13] 'You are the salt of the earth; but if salt has lost its taste, how can its saltiness be restored? It is no longer good for anything, but is thrown out and trampled under foot.

[14] 'You are the light of the world. A city built on a hill cannot be hidden. [15] No one after lighting a lamp puts it under the bushel basket, but on the lampstand, and it gives light to all in the house. [16] In the same way, let your light shine before others, so that they may see your good works and give glory to your Father in heaven.

[17] 'Do not think that I have come to abolish the law or the prophets; I have come not to abolish but to fulfil. [18] For truly I tell you, until heaven and earth pass away, not one letter, not one stroke of a letter, will pass from the law until all is accomplished. [19] Therefore, whoever breaks one of the least of these commandments, and teaches others to do the same, will be called least in the kingdom of heaven; but whoever does them and teaches them will be called great in the kingdom of heaven. [20] For I tell you, unless your righteousness exceeds that of the scribes and Pharisees, you will never enter the kingdom of heaven.'

Opposite: The Sermon on the Mount, by Fra Angelico (1387-1455)

Understand the Word of God

This session will explore:

- ❖ The Sermon on the Mount as the basic law of Christianity
- ❖ How Matthew sees obedience to the Law of Christ
- ❖ The qualities needed for 'righteousness'
- ❖ The criticism of the Pharisees in Matthew's gospel

Setting in the Gospel

From Mark the reader gets a strong impression of the personality of Jesus, but perhaps less of his teaching. The Gospel according to Matthew supplements this. It is as though Matthew's community had come to him and said, 'We want to know more of the actual teaching of Jesus.' Matthew responded by giving what was either his own gathering of the teaching of Jesus or a collection of sayings of Jesus, used also by Luke.

Matthew and Luke arranged these sayings in a different order, Matthew making them into five great discourses, of which this Sermon on the Mount is the first. Matthew represents Jesus as seated on the mountain to teach his new Law, just as Moses was imagined seated on Mount Sinai to give the Law, but we do not need to suppose that Jesus gave all these teachings on one occasion. It would have been indigestible!

Matthew was a methodical teacher. He gathers together Jesus' teaching on the different aspects of the community, which is to show in its manner of life, and to proclaim to the world, the Sovereignty of God. The arrangement of the five discourses can be seen as a *chiasmus* (a-b-c-b-a), each discourse showing a different aspect of the Kingdom or Kingship of God.

Chiasmus, a balancing figure much used in ancient literature, is frequent in the gospels. The chiasmus has been compared to an onion, if you cut the onion down the middle. The first phrase balances the last, the second balances the second-last, and so on. The heart and climax of the figure is in the middle.

Matthew always uses the expression 'Kingdom of Heaven', rather than 'Kingdom of God'. He has the Jewish instinct of reverence for God and so, instead of over-using the divine name, he uses the place where God is enthroned, heaven. Out of reverence Jews never pronounce God's personal name, revealed to Moses in Exodus 3:14. Its four letters are YHWH. It is too sacred to be spoken. In worship, the word 'Adonai' ('the Lord') is substituted. Outside the synagogue Jews simply use the expression 'the Name'. Many Jews these days write 'G-d' to avoid the pronunciation of that word.

What Kind of Text?

Matthew was writing the gospel for a community of Christians sprung from Judaism, where the Jewish Law was still observed, but with a distinctly Christian emphasis. The Sermon on the Mount may be regarded as the Christian version of the Law, for it is in the Sermon on the Mount that Matthew shows most clearly what was Jesus' special emphasis. It

This hill is a suggested location of the Sermon on the Mount. Once known as Mt. Eremos, this hill is located between Capernaum and Tabgha and is just above the 'Cove of the Sower.'

begins with the Beatitudes, which teach the basic attitudes needed to attract God's blessing. Other sayings follow, about salt and light, and about fulfilment. At the end of our passage, in verse 20, Matthew gives one great principle, that of a greater righteousness, which he illustrates in the rest of chapter 5 with six ways in which Jesus' teaching on the Law surpasses that of current interpretations.

In chapter 6, as the Sermon on the Mount continues, Matthew teaches how a Christian should practise the classic Jewish good works of almsgiving, prayer and fasting. He starts with the principle in verse 1, that good works should not be paraded, which is then applied to each good work in turn. Finally, chapter 7 is focussed on trust in God, and ends the Sermon with some pairs of images about success and failure (7:13-27).

Commentary: verse by verse reading

The Beatitudes

v.1 Jesus is seated on the holy mountain, wherever that may be. Holy Land guides blithely point out the hill above the lakeside village of Capernaum. Jesus assumes the position of Moses, who taught the Law from the holy mountain.

v.2 Matthew begins with eight Beatitudes, while in Luke 6 there are only four. Matthew teaches the basic attitudes needed for the Kingdom ('poor *in spirit*', 'hunger and thirst *for righteousness*'), whereas Luke shows Jesus pronouncing God's blessing on those who are actually poor, hungry and thirsty, in a similar fashion to Matthew 5:11-12, where there is a blessing on those who are being persecuted. Matthew's eight are beautifully arranged so that they become easier to remember: at first and last the blessing is 'for the Kingdom of heaven is theirs', to show that this is all about God's kingdom or kingship. Both the first group of four and the second group end with 'righteousness', a legal term, to show that this is the way to observe the Law. In the Greek text there is also a neat chiastic balance in the number of words used.

The Beatitude-formula is traditional in Judaism, frequent in the Psalms (*Psalms* 1 and 118) and in Jewish wisdom-writings (*Proverbs* 3:13). It is not about the 'feel-good factor', saying that the person is happy or contented. God's blessing is not about immediate satisfaction, for there may yet be plenty of struggles and hardship in the Lord's service. Rather it is a promise of God's affectionate regard, special care and ultimate reward. Those who are blessed are, despite their sufferings from persecution, contempt, hunger and thirst, safe in God's hands.

v.3 The first condition for receiving God's blessing of the kingdom is to realise that one needs it. Poverty of spirit is avoidance of all complacency, an openness to God, and a realisation of dependence on the divine generosity. It is the awareness of reliance on God, open-handed and open-hearted, an attitude engendered particularly by the prophets in the dark days of the return from exile, when the people's high hopes of triumph and independence seemed repeatedly to be disappointed.

v.4 Comfort for those who mourn is another strong theme in the prophets. Isaiah 40: 1-2 reads: 'Comfort, o comfort my people, says your God. Speak tenderly to Jerusalem, and cry to her that she has served her term, that her penalty is paid, that she has received from the Lord's hand double for all her sins.'

v.5 The third beatitude is similar to, indeed almost an amplification of the first, and in some texts comes immediately after the first. Again, it is difficult to translate, for 'meekness' is often seen as weakness, a misplaced gentleness. The quality recommended is firmer, a lack of pomposity. Jesus uses the same word when he declares himself to be 'meek/gentle and humble of heart' (*Matthew* 11:29), and again is the 'meek/humble' king who rides into Jerusalem on a donkey rather than a warhorse (*Matthew* 21).

v.6 'Righteousness' is a tricky word, which has fallen out of common speech, and is often associated with that unpleasant quality, self-righteousness. In Christian writings based on Judaism (such especially as Matthew and Paul) 'righteousness' means two things. The first sense is used overwhelmingly by Paul, the second by Matthew.

Firstly, God's saving gift of standing right with God, that is, God's acceptance of human beings in fulfilment of the promise to Abraham, about which St Paul writes: 'Abraham trusted in God and it was reckoned to him as righteousness.' (*Romans* 4:3) In this case righteousness is a free gift from God. All human beings can do is trust in God's promises.

Secondly, righteousness is the loving human response to God's loving gift of the Law, the attempt to thank God for this gift by fulfilling the requirements of the Law, that is, by obedience to the Law.

v.7 Another misunderstood quality is 'mercy'. This translates the wonderful Hebrew concept of *hesed*, love, in the sense of attentiveness to the needs of others, a generosity in self-giving, no matter what the cost, the sort of love one seeks in the family. I may not get on very well with my siblings/parents/children, but in the last analysis they can be sure of my vigorous help.

Matthew repeats three times the principle drawn from scripture, 'What I want is mercy/love/*hesed* not sacrifice' (*Hosea* 6:6, given by Matthew in 9:13, 12:7 and 23:23). This is the quality needed for real observance of God's Law.

v.8 The pure in heart shall see God. About seeing God St Irenaeus says: 'Man cannot see God and live. But because of God's love and goodness toward us, and because God can do all things, he goes so far as to grant those who love him the privilege of seeing him.' (*Adversus haereses* 4.20.5.)

v.9 Peace is one of the principal constituents of the kingship of God, not merely absence of strife and of war, but a positive healing, bonding and unitive factor. 'Peace'/*shalom* is a frequent Jewish greeting, but it has special significance in the messianic context of a kingdom of peace, where the wolf will live with the lamb (*Isaiah* 11:6-9) and swords be beaten into ploughshares, where the first greeting of missioners is 'peace' (*Matthew* 10:13), and where peace features largely in all Paul's letters, not only in the initial greetings, but the relationships between the members of Christ's body, the Church. So making peace is one of the principal tasks of the Christian.

v.10 The eighth Beatitude once again speaks of 'righteousness'.

vv.11-12 At the end of the Beatitudes Matthew adds another saying on persecution, which is similar to Luke's Beatitudes. He is well aware that persecution will be the lot of all faithful Christians. It is ironical that in Matthew's community the persecution seems to have been mostly from fellow-Jews who did not accept Jesus as Messiah. The prophets too were persecuted by their own people, as Matthew comments.

Whatever we do, we shall no longer be seeking any of those things when we reach the vision of God. Indeed, what should one search for when one has God before one's eyes? Or what would satisfy one who would not be satisfied with God? Yes, we wish to see God. Who does not have this desire? We strive to see God. We are on fire with the desire of seeing God. Unless your heart is pure you will not be permitted to see what cannot be seen unless the heart be pure.

(St Augustine, Sermon 53.6.)

Salt and Light

vv.13-16 Matthew often uses images in pairs (wolves posing as sheep, building a house on rock or on sand, the treasure and the pearl of great price). He does the same here, drawing the images of salt and light from different contexts in Mark (*Mark* 9:50 and 4:21). Both in different ways are images of giving savour and clarity, where there is otherwise only insipidity and darkness. We can see Jesus doing this in all his activity, but to imitate this requires sensitivity, inspiration and courage. Perhaps, rather than striving to do this as individuals, it is better to play our part in the Church's efforts in this direction!

Salt adds the sensation of hidden flavour. Likewise the apostles are preachers of surprising heavenly things and eternity. Like sowers, they sow immortality on all bodies on which their discourse has been sprinkled. So those who are to be salted with the power of gospel teaching have rightly been called the salt of the earth. They are already being preserved to the end.

(St Hilary, on Matthew 4.10.)

Let those you illumine by the light of your words be seasoned by the salt of your works. For the one who teaches, and practises what he teaches, teaches truly. But one who does not practise what he teaches does not teach anyone but casts a bad light on himself.

(Anonymous homily on Matthew, PG 56.687.)

The Law and the Prophets

2 Corinthians 1:19-20 reads:

'For the Son of God, Jesus Christ, whom we proclaimed among you, was not 'Yes and No'; but in him it is always 'Yes'. For in him every one of God's promises is a 'Yes'.'

'Not one letter, not one stroke of a letter' is literally 'not an iota, not a horn'. Iota is the smallest letter, hardly more than a dot. A horn is a mere decorative flourish at the extremity of a letter.

The Law of the Gospel fulfils, refines, surpasses and leads the Old Law to its perfection. In the Beatitudes the New Law fulfils the divine promises by elevating and orienting them towards the 'kingdom of heaven'. It is addressed to those open to accepting this new hope with faith, and so marks out the surprising ways of the Kingdom.

(Catechism of the Catholic Church 1967)

vv.17-19 This paragraph is in a way the key to the chapter, or even to the whole moral teaching of the Sermon on the Mount, or even of the gospel itself. Matthew's message is that Jesus is the completion of the story of Israel, or – as Paul puts it – the 'Amen', or the 'Yes', to the promises God made to Abraham.

The Law does not pass away, but in Christianity is brought to completion. This is why Matthew is so determined to show at every turn that the Old Testament is fulfilled. Nor is this foreign to Jesus' own stance. Just as Mary's understanding at the Annunciation that her child would be different from all other children was framed in the Old Testament terms of the promises to David, so Jesus in his childhood will have learnt about God's ways and God's guidance of the people in terms of the Law given to Israel. This was the teaching which had guided Israel to the point where it was ready to receive the Messiah, the final messenger of the Lord.

There was another way in which Jesus was to complete the Law, and this is seen in the six antitheses which follow in verses 21-48. These are phrased: 'You have heard it said….. But I say this….' Jesus quotes the Law and then perfects it in various ways which make it more total, sometimes more demanding, sometimes more fulfilling. Each one is different, but all show Jesus' sovereign understanding and command of the Law itself, a mastery which is already an indication of his divine status, for no one can change God's Law but God alone.

v.20 This verse, which ends this section, is also the principle governing the next section, the antitheses which show that current interpretations (and even in some cases current regulations) of the Law have not yet attained perfection. In the background is also the strife against the Pharisees which is so prominent in Matthew.

Jesus himself was at least in some ways close to the Pharisees. He and they held that the completion of the kingship of God would consist in perfect obedience to the Law. Their only difference from Jesus in this was that he and they interpreted this perfection in different ways.

Jesus often has different solutions to moral problems from those of the Pharisees, but they are reached by the same methods of argument. It was not the Pharisees who had Jesus executed, for they appear nowhere in the Passion Narrative, and seem to have stayed clear of the whole process.

As we have seen, Matthew insists that his community sees in Jesus the fulfilment of Judaism. However, constantly in the background of Matthew's Gospel is strife between Matthew's community and those other Jews, who did not recognise Jesus as the Messiah. Now, by the time Matthew came to write, after the destruction of Jerusalem in 70 AD, the Judaism of the Pharisees was the only surviving strand of Judaism. The Sadducees and the Essenes were destroyed by the Romans in the Sack of Jerusalem. So at the time of Matthew it is the Pharisees who are the chief opponents of Christianity, and the hostility between Matthew's Christian Jewish community and these non-Christian Jews is palpable.

The Sermon on the Mount, from the Sistine Chapel, c.1481-83 (fresco), Rosselli, Cosimo (1439-1507).

A recent document of the Pontifical Biblical Commission reads:

Which was the most important religious group during Jesus' public life? Josephus says that the Pharisees were the main party, extremely influential in the towns. It was perhaps for this reason that Jesus is presented more often in conflict with them than with any other group, an indirect acknowledgement of their importance. Furthermore, this party within Judaism survived better than the others and nascent Christianity had to confront it.

(The Jewish People and their Sacred Scriptures in the Christian Bible 67)

The Word Lives on

This opening part of the Sermon on the Mount is read in the liturgy on the Fourth, Fifth and Sixth Sundays of Ordinary Time in Year A, the year of Matthew.

It is also read on weekdays during the tenth week of Ordinary Time.

The Beatitudes of Matthew are the gospel reading for the Solemnity of All Saints on November 1st. They may also be selected for Masses of Holy Men and Women, for the Sacrament of Confirmation, and for Weddings or Funeral Masses.

The words of Jesus encouraging disciples to be like salt and light, in Matthew 5:13-16, may be read in Masses of Doctors of the Church, of Holy Men and Women, at Ordinations to the Priesthood, and also at Weddings.

Church of the Beatitudes, above Sea of Galilee.

Live the Word of God

Listen again to the reading: Matthew 5:1-20

What do you hear now?

Suggestions for reflection and prayer

Where do I place my beatitude? Is the blessing of God my deepest desire? How do I set about getting it?

Run through the beatitudes and ask yourself how you measure up to each of the qualities.

Do I regard God's Law as a constricting obligation or as a precious gift and way of coming nearer to God?

How do I see righteousness, as a free gift from God or as obedience to God's Law?

❖ Pray individually for each of the qualities featured in the Beatitudes.

❖ Pray for greater understanding between Christians and Jews, for genuine willingness on both sides to understand the point of view of the others.

❖ Pray that we may learn to observe the Law with both fidelity and love, and to understand how both may be married together.

The Beatitudes depict the countenance of Jesus Christ and portray his charity. They are the paradoxical promises that sustain hope in the midst of tribulations; they proclaim the blessings and rewards already secured, however dimly, for Christ's disciples. (Catechism of the Catholic Church 1717)

The Wonders of Jesus

Hear the Word of God

Read: Matthew 8:23-9:8

8 [23] And when he got into the boat, his disciples followed him. [24] A gale arose on the lake, so great that the boat was being swamped by the waves; but he was asleep. [25] And they went and woke him up, saying, 'Lord, save us! We are perishing!' [26] And he said to them, 'Why are you afraid, you of little faith?' Then he got up and rebuked the winds and the sea; and there was a dead calm. [27] They were amazed, saying, 'What sort of man is this, that even the winds and the sea obey him?'

[28] When he came to the other side, to the country of the Gadarenes, two demoniacs coming out of the tombs met him. They were so fierce that no one could pass that way. [29] Suddenly they shouted, 'What have you to do with us, Son of God? Have you come here to torment us before the time?' [30] Now a large herd of swine was feeding at some distance from them. [31] The demons begged him, 'If you cast us out, send us into the herd of swine.' [32] And he said to them, 'Go!' So they came out and entered the swine; and suddenly, the whole herd rushed down the steep bank into the lake and perished in the water. [33] The swineherds ran off, and on going into the town, they told the whole story about what had happened to the demoniacs. [34] Then the whole town came out to meet Jesus; and when they saw him, they begged him to leave their neighbourhood. 9 [1] And after getting into a boat he crossed the water and came to his own town.

[2] And just then some people were carrying a paralysed man lying on a bed. When Jesus saw their faith, he said to the paralytic, 'Take heart, son; your sins are forgiven.' [3] Then some of the scribes said to themselves, 'This man is blaspheming.' [4] But Jesus, perceiving their thoughts, said, 'Why do you think evil in your hearts? [5] For which is easier, to say, 'Your sins are forgiven', or to say, 'Stand up and walk'? [6] But so that you may know that the Son of Man has authority on earth to forgive sins' — he then said to the paralytic — 'Stand up, take your bed and go to your home.' [7] And he stood up and went to his home. [8] When the crowds saw it, they were filled with awe, and they glorified God, who had given such authority to human beings.

Opposite: Jesus Calms the Storm, 1995, by Laura James, (Contemporary Artist)

Understand the Word of God

This session will explore:

- ❖ The concept and historicity of the miracles of Jesus
- ❖ The wonders and the Kingdom of God
- ❖ Forgiveness of sins
- ❖ Titles of Jesus: Son of God, son of man

Setting in the Gospel

Matthew's gospel is divided into five 'books', each consisting of a narrative section and a discourse. Before these five comes the Infancy Narrative, and after them comes the Narrative of the Passion, Death and Resurrection. The chiastic pattern of the Discourses has been set out above, in the previous section. The narrative section of this second 'book' of the gospel consists of ten miracles. The methodical Matthew has gathered together ten miracles to show one way in which Jesus brings the sovereignty of God to a new intensity by healing, forgiveness and deliverance from fear and trouble. This follows the Sermon on the Mount, for which Matthew had gathered sayings which show what is involved in fulfilling the will of God, expressed in this new Law of God.

There were at the time many different expectations of the Kingdom or Kingship or Sovereignty of God. Some saw it in political terms, the forcible expulsion of the Roman occupying powers, for God could not be acknowledged as King while the Emperor was 'lord'. Jesus was wholly concentrated on bringing the sovereignty of God to reality, and the urgency of its coming. He saw it, however, primarily in terms of healing of souls and bodies.

The Pharisees, who were so preoccupied with observance of the Law, saw the Kingdom in terms of perfect obedience to God's Law (a conception which Jesus must have shared, to judge from his careful re-interpretation of how the Law must be obeyed). The Essenes, waiting on the shore of the Dead Sea for the coming of the Kingdom, saw it in terms of the violent destruction of the 'sons of darkness' by the 'sons of light', led by the Messiah. John the Baptist saw it in terms of the axe put to the root of rotten trees, or the gathering of wheat into barns and burning of the useless chaff.

(Matthew 3:10 Luke 3:17).

The ten miracles are divided into groups of 3-3-4, interspersed with two passages on discipleship and the commitment required (8:18-22; 9:9-17), for, especially in Matthew, the disciples are very much involved in the miracles, and will continue to spread the kingship of God through their own similar action. In addition, Matthew characteristically includes a quotation from Isaiah (*Isaiah* 53:4 in *Matthew* 8:17), to underline that by these miracles Jesus fulfils the scriptures which express the hopes of Israel.

After the Miracle of the Evil Spirits Turned into Swine, Italian School, (15th century).

What Kind of Text?

Quite simply, our passage consists of three miracle-stories, a particular kind of narrative which has its own characteristics. The modern word 'miracle' is not particularly apt, for it places the emphasis on the fact that what occurred was against the laws of nature. The Hebrew had no such concept as 'the laws of nature', and considered not so much the contradiction of nature as that these events were manifestations of the wonderful power of God, working to protect God's people in their hour of need, rather after the model of the wonders of the exodus from Egypt, when God protected Israel through all the vicissitudes and difficulties of forty years in the desert. There were a number of claimants to be Messiah around the time of Jesus, and they all (according to the Jewish historian Josephus) claimed to be able to repeat the wonders of the exodus and of Moses, as part of their authentication. Most of them were destroyed by the Romans before they got a chance!

Go and tell John what you hear and see: the blind receive their sight, the lame walk, the lepers are cleansed, the deaf hear, the dead are raised, and the poor have good news brought to them.

(Matthew 11:4-5)

Most of these claimants promised to repeat the more public and militaristic miracles of the exodus. In the case of Jesus there is an additional element. Throughout the period of the prophets, especially from Isaiah onwards, Israel had expected the sovereignty of the Lord to be manifested in the end-times by an era of safety and tranquillity, when Israel would live in the serene peace of the Lord. Isaiah prophesied this in the lovely passage 11:1-9, when the wolf would live with the lamb and the lion eat hay like an ox – no more strife and bloodshed. A later chapter of Isaiah takes this up with 'the eyes of the blind will be opened, the ears of the deaf unsealed' (*Isaiah* 35:5), and the Third Part of Isaiah with 'He has sent me to bring good news to the afflicted' (*Isaiah* 61:1) – passages to which Jesus alludes when he is sending news to John the Baptist to explain his own activity (*Matthew* 11:2-6). These wonders therefore are the beginning of the inauguration of the reign of God in the world.

Did the miracles really happen? The exorcisms were accepted even by Jesus' enemies, who tried to explain them away as evidence that Jesus was in league with Satan, the prince of devils (Matthew 12:24). Many of the cures are of psycho-somatic illnesses, which were often – in the primitive state of medicine at the time – explained as possession by evil spirits. We have no right to limit the reaction of those who suffered from such diseases when confronted with the towering and awesome holiness of Jesus. We cannot limit the effect produced by confrontation with the man who was also divine.

Commentary: verse by verse reading

The Calming of the Storm

v.23 Some of the miracles are shaped to bring out their similarity to Old Testament stories. In the Old Testament God is represented as dominating the seas. God alone has power over the waters, which so often in the Old Testament represent the dark forces of chaos, threatening to engulf the world. This narrative can therefore be regarded as a testimony that Jesus is this God who controls the forces of creation.

Matthew is very conscious of the disciples and always mentions them, whereas Mark, from whom Matthew derives his account, merely leaves it impersonal (*Mark* 4:36). As we shall see, here as elsewhere, Mark is quite critical of the disciples, a criticism which Matthew weakens. For Matthew the disciples are always working with their Master.

vv.24-26 In Matthew the disturbance on the sea is far greater than in Mark, literally 'a great earthquake arose on the lake'. While in Mark the disciples are sarcastic to Jesus ('Don't you care?'), in Matthew their response is model, 'Lord, save us!'; they call him 'Lord' and show the confidence of the ideal disciple in his power to save. So Jesus' rebuke is less severe: 'you of little faith!' instead of Mark's exasperated 'Have you still no faith?' Matthew tends to be aware that the disciples are the future respected leaders of the community, and treats them gently. In the later community of disciples Jesus will be present where two or three are gathered together (*Matthew* 18:20), and it is as though they already recognise this presence.

v.27 Again, while in Mark the disciples are very frightened by Jesus' power over the elements, they do not seem to understand, and merely say 'Who is this?' (*Mark* 4:41), in Matthew's account they are 'amazed' and say 'What sort of person is this?' There is more suggestion of appreciation of the quality of Jesus, of his amazing authority, rather than simply the fear and puzzlement in Mark.

Psalm 65:7 You silence the roaring of the seas, the roaring of their waves.

Psalm 89:9 You rule the raging of the sea; when its waves rise, you still them.

Psalm 107:29 He made the storm be still, and the waves of the sea were hushed.

Before the tempest of the waters he stills the tempests in their souls. He admonishes them, 'Why are you afraid, you of little faith?' He instructs them about the way human fear comes from weakness of mind, not from the actual approach of threatening trials.

(John Chrysostom, PG 57.351)

Jesus Heals the Gadarene Demoniacs

Matthew 14:33 And those in the boat worshipped him, saying, 'Truly you are the Son of God.'

Matthew 16:16 Simon Peter answered, 'You are the Messiah, the Son of the living God.'

He lived among the tombs and no one could restrain him any more. He had often been restrained with shackles and chains, but the chains he wrenched apart, and the shackles he broke in pieces, and no one had the strength to subdue him

(Mark 5:3-4).

v.28 Where did this happen? Mark puts it at Gerasa (modern Jerash), which is some 30 km from the Lake of Galilee. Matthew puts it at Gadara, which is only 10 km distant, but still a long run for a pig. Both are in the region of the hellenised cities, the Decapolis on the east of the Jordan. The early biblical scholar Origen thought it happened at a place now called El-Kursi, which has the same consonants as 'Gerasa', and is conveniently placed on top of a high cliff just a few metres from the eastern shore of the Lake.

v.29 The evil spirits are more perceptive than human beings, even than the disciples. In Old Testament usage Israel is described as God's son. So are the angels, and the dynasty of Davidic kings. In Jesus' time, then, it means someone united to God by special bonds of affection and closeness, entrusted by God with a special mission and empowered to carry it out. It does not yet convey fully 'the incarnate Son of God', as it will in John. In Mark the first human being to acknowledge Jesus as 'son of God' is the centurion at the foot of the Cross. In Matthew there are earlier acknowledgements. The synoptic evangelists may be on the way to giving this title the fuller sense it will bear in John.

What do the spirits mean by 'before the time'? The same expression occurs in Matthew 26:18, 'My time is near.' It may be an indication that the time when Jesus will definitively conquer the powers of evil is at the crucifixion and resurrection.

vv.30-32 The point of the 2,000 suicidal swine (numbered in *Mark* 5:13, not Matthew or Luke) is, of course, to stress the vicious, destructive power of the evil spirits. This may also be the reason why Matthew doubles the single victim to 'two demoniacs' and makes them actively harmful and aggressive to passers-by, instead of being merely one unfortunate victim of self-harm. Mark's description of the pathetic sufferer is more tragic and more graphic than Matthew's.

vv.33-34 This incident is Jesus' first contact with gentiles since the magi did him homage, his first sally into gentile territory. This is a fascinating meeting, for the expression translated 'to meet him' suggests a solemn procession out of the city to greet an emperor; it is used of an official delegation to welcome the emperor. However, they are obviously not yet ready to receive Jesus. The mission to 'all nations' will begin only after the resurrection (*Matthew* 28:19), for first – especially in Matthew – Jesus must offer the good news to 'the house of Israel' (*Matthew* 10:5-6).

They entreat him to leave their district, not out of pride on their part (as many believe), but out of humility. They judge themselves unworthy of the Lord's presence, just as Peter after the catch of fish fell before the Saviour's knees and said, 'Depart from me, for I am a sinner'.

(Jerome, CCL 9a, 409)

The Two Men Possessed with Unclean Spirits, illustration for 'The Life of Christ', c.1884-96 by JJ Tissot.

Jesus Heals a Paralytic

9:1-2 Mark's account of this story reads: 'When they could not bring him to Jesus because of the crowd, they removed the roof above him, and after having dug through it, they let down the mat on which the paralytic lay.' (*Mark* 2:4) In Matthew there is no mention of house or roof, and in general much less detail. Matthew is interested in Jesus' power, not in the delightful, dramatic story told in Mark of the crowd blocking the entrance, and the sick man's team scrabbling their way in through the feebly-built roof.

More surprisingly, Matthew abbreviates the story so much that he does not even give us the evidence of their faith; it almost seems as though they were just carrying the man and bumped into Jesus. However, it is striking that Jesus does not ask for repentance or contrition from the sick man; 'seeing their faith' he simply offers forgiveness, or, even more, simply says that the man's sins have been forgiven. All the emphasis is on forgiveness, beside which the physical healing becomes insignificant. Forgiveness freely offered is a key note of this gospel.

vv.3-5 The scribes are perfectly correct: human beings can forgive offences committed one against another, but only God can forgive the guilt. I can pardon you for stealing from me, but you are still guilty of the theft. Jesus shows his quality also by reading their minds.

v.6 'Son of man' is Jesus' preferred way of referring to himself. It is a mysterious expression, probably a reticent way of referring to oneself without pushing oneself forward, equivalent to 'one' or sometimes 'yours truly' in English. Basically it means 'a human being', but in stories of about this time some rabbis use it to refer to themselves.

Jesus was chary of accepting the title 'Messiah' because of its political implications. He refers to himself as 'son of man' in claiming authority (here and 12:8) and in the three great prophecies of the Passion (16:21, 17:22-23, 20:17-19). The evangelists also see in it an allusion to the great vision of the son of man in Daniel 7:13-14, but it is uncertain whether this connotation was in Jesus' own mind. The text of Daniel

Earlier in the gospel, the son to be born is to be named 'Jesus' because he will save his people from their sins (1:21). Jesus calls the unclean tax-collector, Matthew (9:9), and joins in a banquet with sinners, not previously demanding that they repent (9:13). Faith is the only pre-condition of Jesus doing anything to help: faith precedes the action, and is strengthened by it. At Nazareth 'he did not do many deeds of power, because of their unbelief' (13:58).

This excerpt from the Jewish Talmud gives an illustration of the use of the phrase 'son of man' by Rabbi Simeon ben Yohai:

Having decided to escape from the cave he sat down at the entrance to the cave. There he saw a fowler trying to catch birds. He heard a heavenly voice say 'Release!' and the bird escaped. Then he said, 'Not even a bird perishes without the will of Heaven. How much less the son of man.'

(Tractate Shebi'ith 38d)

reads as follows: 'I saw one like a son of man coming with the clouds of heaven. And he came to the Ancient One and was presented before him. To him was given dominion and glory and kingship, that all peoples, nations and languages should serve him.'

vv.7-8 The response of the onlookers is an awe at the divine. In Mark this is even more striking, because it comes as the climax of a day of Jesus' activity at Capernaum, where his authority becomes more and more impressive. Matthew rearranges the order of incidents to make his collection of miracles. He says that they glorified God for giving such authority to human beings. Why the plural? It is probably to draw attention to the fact that Jesus not only forgives sins on earth, but also imparts to Peter (16:19) and to his Church (18:18) his divine authority to forgive sins.

Icon depicting the Healing of the Paralytic, 1811, Bulgarian School, (19th century).

The Word Lives on

These miracle-stories are never read on Sundays, possibly because the parallel accounts in Mark of the healing of the paralytic and the calming of the storm are read on Sundays in the Year of Mark. The passages in Matthew are heard as part of the continuous reading of the Gospel of Matthew on weekdays. They feature on the Tuesday, Wednesday and Thursday of the Thirteenth Week of the Year.

Jesus heals the paralysed Man by Jesus Mafa.

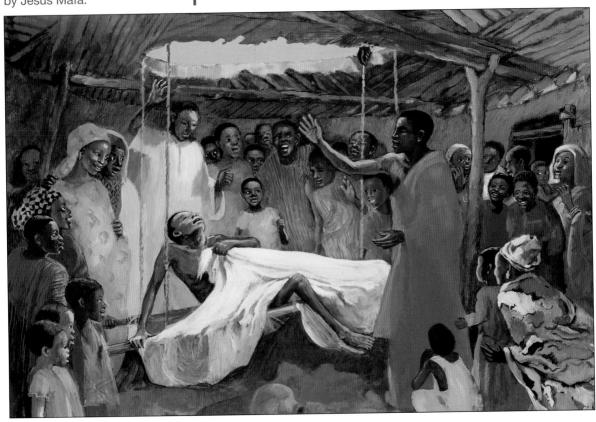

Live the Word of God

Listen again to the reading: Matthew 8:23-9:8

What do you hear now?

Suggestions for reflection and prayer

What are the storms in my life? Do I submit them to the Lord and trust the Lord to look after my leaky boat?

Is there any way in which I am possessed by evil, an evil that I cannot shake off, or even do not really want to shake off?

Do I come to Jesus to be healed? Do I frankly and faithfully acknowledge to myself and to the Lord my failings, my wounds and my distortions?

What is there that I have not forgiven, and whom have I not forgiven, so that this is blocking my own forgiveness?

- ❖ Pray for the sick, especially those suffering from psychological illnesses, who often get less sympathy than those whose sickness is physical.
- ❖ Pray for those who are caught in unexpected storms and crises and especially those who need to help others through such crises.
- ❖ Pray for a strong and unwavering faith, and for trust in the Lord, who will look after us however foolish and unreliable we are.

Jesus is as saddened by the 'lack of faith' of his own neighbours and the 'little faith' of his own disciples as he is struck with admiration at the great faith of the Roman centurion and the Canaanite woman.

(Catechism of the Catholic Church 2610)

The Mission of the Disciples

Hear the Word of God

Read: Matthew 9:36-10:20

9 [36] When he saw the crowds, he had compassion for them, because they were harassed and helpless, like sheep without a shepherd. [37] Then he said to his disciples, 'The harvest is plentiful, but the labourers are few; [38] therefore ask the Lord of the harvest to send out labourers into his harvest.'

10 [1] Then Jesus summoned his twelve disciples and gave them authority over unclean spirits, to cast them out, and to cure every disease and every sickness. [2] These are the names of the twelve apostles: first, Simon, also known as Peter, and his brother Andrew; James son of Zebedee, and his brother John; [3] Philip and Bartholomew; Thomas and Matthew the tax-collector; James son of Alphaeus, and Thaddaeus; [4] Simon the Cananaean, and Judas Iscariot, the one who betrayed him.

[5] These twelve Jesus sent out with the following instructions: 'Go nowhere among the Gentiles, and enter no town of the Samaritans, [6] but go rather to the lost sheep of the house of Israel. [7] As you go, proclaim the good news, 'The kingdom of heaven has come near.' [8] Cure the sick, raise the dead, cleanse the lepers, cast out demons. You received without payment; give without payment. [9] Take no gold, or silver, or copper in your belts, [10] no bag for your journey, or two tunics, or sandals, or a staff; for labourers deserve their food. [11] Whatever town or village you enter, find out who in it is worthy, and stay there until you leave. [12] As you enter the house, greet it. [13] If the house is worthy, let your peace come upon it; but if it is not worthy, let your peace return to you. [14] If anyone will not welcome you or listen to your words, shake off the dust from your feet as you leave that house or town. [15] Truly I tell you, it will be more tolerable for the land of Sodom and Gomorrah on the day of judgement than for that town.

[16] 'See, I am sending you out like sheep into the midst of wolves; so be wise as serpents and innocent as doves. [17] Beware of them, for they will hand you over to councils and flog you in their synagogues; [18] and you will be dragged before governors and kings because of me, as a testimony to them and the Gentiles. [19] When they hand you over, do not worry about how you are to speak or what you are to say; for what you are to say will be given to you at that time; [20] for it is not you who speak, but the Spirit of your Father speaking through you'.

Opposite: Plaque depicting Christ blessing the Apostles, Constantinople.

Understand the Word of God

This session will explore:

❖ The importance of the Twelve in Matthew

❖ The new Christian family of those who remain loyal to Christ

❖ The activity of the Spirit in the mission of the Church

Setting in the Gospel

This passage contains a large part of the second of Matthew's five great discourses. As pointed out earlier, these discourses consider the Kingdom or Sovereignty of God. This second discourse is about the community proclaiming the Kingdom, and balances the fourth discourse, in Matthew chapter 18, which is about relationships within the community. After listing the Twelve, in a passage dependent on Mark, though in this gospel 'Levi' is replaced by 'Matthew', Matthew has gathered together a collection of sayings of Jesus giving guidance for the proclamation of the Kingdom, and about its challenges and dangers. Matthew is a methodical teacher, and likes to bring together all the teachings of Jesus on one particular subject.

Prominent in the background of Matthew's gospel is the controversy between Christian Jews and those Jews who had not accepted Jesus as the Messiah. The hostility is constantly simmering just below the surface, and occasionally comes out: 'they will hand you over to councils and will flog you in their synagogues' (10:16).

What kind of text?

Being one of Matthew's five great discourses, this is composed of sayings of Jesus collected by Matthew. The overwhelming majority of these come also in Mark or – according to the majority view of scholars – in the lost collection of sayings called 'Q' (for the German '*die Quelle*' = the Source), which was known also to Luke. The exact similarity of Matthew and Luke over large areas suggests that both evangelists were using the same document, either written down or carefully learnt by heart and remembered. The discourse is carefully marked off by the evangelist at beginning and end. It is preceded in 9:35 by the same summary statement as was used in 4:23, before the Sermon on the Mount. In 11:1 we find the same conclusion as was used for the Sermon on the Mount in 7:28.

Ezekiel 34: 11 For thus says the Lord God: I myself will search for my sheep, and will seek them out.

Psalm 23:1 1 The Lord is my shepherd, I shall not want.

John 10:11 Jesus says: I am the good shepherd. The good shepherd lays down his life for the sheep.

Those who with God's help have welcomed Christ's call and freely responded to it are urged on by love of Christ to proclaim the Good News everywhere in the world. All Christ's faithful are called to hand it on from generation to generation, by professing the faith, by living it in fraternal sharing and by celebrating it in liturgy and prayer.

(Catechism of the Catholic Church 3)

Commentary: verse by verse reading

The Compassion of Jesus

v.36 This note on Jesus' sympathy for the shepherdless crowds is given by Mark just before the Feeding of the Five Thousand (*Mark* 6:34). It is perhaps significant of the different approaches of the two evangelists that in Mark Jesus feeds the crowds with food and in Matthew with teaching! The comment is also rich in allusion, for in the Old Testament God is the shepherd of his people. In the New Testament this is applied to Jesus.

v.37 In John 4:35-38, at the end of the scene with the Samaritan woman, the same image of labourers sent to the harvest is used. There, however, it has more urgency, for the fields are 'white for the harvest'. Such urgency was a feature of Jesus' proclamation: 'The kingship of God has come near' or 'is imminent'. Here, in Matthew, it seems less pressing, for Matthew is envisaging the proclamation to the world up to the time of the final coming of Christ.

The Call of the Disciples

vv.1-4 The most important thing about the list of the Twelve is their number. The names given in different lists vary, but the number is always the same. Even when Judas has left them, they are still known as 'the Twelve'. The importance of the number is as the twelve foundation-stones of the new Israel, corresponding to the number of the original tribes of Israel. This is particularly important to Matthew, for whom the community of the New Israel is an earthly reality, with a structure and an organisation, outlined in the fourth discourse in chapter 18.

Simon Peter is always the first in the lists and clearly has a special position. Mark 6:16 explains that Jesus gave him the additional name of 'Peter' ('*Kepha*' in Aramaic). It means 'Rock', though we do not know why Jesus gave him this name. Was he a large, craggy man? Was he comforting? Reliable and good in a crisis (hardly)? Was it a serious name or friendly mockery? In any case, throughout the Bible the imposition of a name implies that the person naming has some proprietary rights over the person named, and imparts a new function or even nature to this person. Jesus and Peter must have known each other well.

The Twelve are to be the judges of the twelve tribes of the New Israel (19:28). The all-powerful Christ is present in his Church, and has given it authority to bind and to loose (9:8 and 18:18). The chosen disciples also play a part in the healing-wonders (15:23). Frequently, Matthew softens or even removes the abrasive criticism of the Twelve by Jesus which Mark stresses. References to their 'hardened hearts' in Mark 6:52 and 8:17, for example, are not repeated by Matthew.

Matthew 16:18-19 And I tell you, you are Peter, and on this rock I will build my church, and the gates of Hades will not prevail against it. I will give you the keys of the kingdom of heaven.

John 1:42 You are Simon son of John. You are to be called Cephas (which is translated Peter).

Iscariot, the other name of Judas, has long been a puzzle. 'Ish' means 'man'. The name could mean 'man from (the village of) Kerioth', or 'man of lies' (sheqarya), or 'man of the treasury' (sakarioth). See John 12:6.

St Peter's Statue in Rome.

The Mission of the Disciples

St Jerome provides the following comment:

This passage is not contrary to the command given later, 'Go, therefore, and make disciples of all nations.' The former command was given before the resurrection and the latter after the resurrection. It was necessary to announce Christ's first coming to the Jews, lest they have a good excuse for saying that the Lord rejected them. (CCL 77.65)

St Hilary comments on the powers been given to the Twelve:

All the power possessed by the Lord is bestowed on the apostles. Those who were prefigured in the image and likeness of God in Adam have now received the perfect image and likeness of Christ. They have been given powers in no way different from those of the Lord. (SC 254.218)

In Paul's missionary letters peace is frequently to the fore, not only in the greeting at the beginning of every letter, but also strikingly often as a gift from 'the God of peace' (Romans 15:33 and 16:20, 1 Corinthians 7:15 and 14:33, 2 Corinthians 13:11, and Philippians 4:9). Jesus is 'our peace' (Ephesians 2:14, 15, 17), and peace is the fruit of the Spirit (Galatians 5:22).

vv.5-6 Jesus insists strongly that his own mission is only to the house of Israel, both in these verses and in 15:24, where he says: 'I was sent only to the lost sheep of the house of Israel.' Despite these words he does go on to heal the daughter of the Canaanite woman in Matthew 15:28. He also heals the gentile son of the centurion in Matthew 8:13. On the other hand, after his resurrection the disciples are sent out with clear instructions to the whole world (28:16-20), whereas in the gospel of Mark the gentile mission after the resurrection is only implied.

vv.7-10 The poverty prescribed by Matthew is even more extreme than that of Mark, disallowing even sandals and spare tunic, as well as a staff and pack. This cannot be for practical reasons or for the urgency of the mission, for lack of sandals would scarcely speed the missioners. It must be to demonstrate total reliance on God, or perhaps reinforcing the saying that the labourer deserves his keep.

The instructions are also slightly less realistic than Mark's. Mark forbids coppers in the money-belt, suggesting that copper coinage is all there is likely to be (*Mark* 6:8). Luke, writing for a richer society, raises it to silver (*Luke* 9:3). Matthew goes right over the top by forbidding gold and silver as well as copper (verse 9).

vv.11-14 In discussing the Beatitudes we have seen the importance of peace in the Christian message. The blessing of 'peace' is more than the conventional Jewish greeting of 'Shalom!' In Matthew the word comes only in the Beatitudes and in this chapter. The terms of the condemnation are so strong that the rejection of peace must stand for the rejection of the message as a whole, and of the messengers who bring it.

v.15 Sodom and Gomorrah are the type of the sinful city. They are situated at the southern end of the Dead Sea, an area eerily and horrifically barren and still uninhabited (apart from the salt-workers). The story of their destruction is told in Genesis 19, after their crimes have come to a head in an attempted homosexual assault on guests. It is not clear which element of their crime is the more serious, the nature of the sexual assault or the abuse of hospitality.

The lakeside city of Capernaum is compared to Sodom unfavourably in 11:24, for refusing to heed Jesus' message of repentance.

The Gospel of Matthew and the First Letter of Peter are the two New Testament writings which place most emphasis on eternal punishment. Paul and John do not mention it at all, concentrating exclusively on the positive elements of Jesus' triumph. It is part of the contemporary Jewish apocalyptic scenario, and at this time the punishments of Gehenna, the rubbish-dump of Jerusalem, where fires were always burning and the stench was characteristically unpleasant, are much stressed.

Holy Apostles, 1998, by Manolis Grigoreas, (b.1952) (Contemporary Artist).

Persecution to be Expected

v.16 Matthew's delightful use of animal imagery is an important part of his teaching. He loves to use images in pairs, often contrasting pairs, as here sheep and wolves, and serpents and doves. Animal images usually have some obvious symbolism (the pig is unclean, the sparrow is cheap, the moth is destructive). The animals often stand for some obvious trait of human behaviour: the hen is motherly, the sheep is gormless. This adds greatly to the effectiveness of his teaching, and may partly explain why, from the second century onwards, Matthew seems to have been the most popular of the gospels.

vv.17-20 Persecution will be the lot not merely of the Twelve but of all those who carry the message of Christ. The perspective here becomes wider than the first mission of the disciples during Jesus' lifetime. Most of this passage is taken over by Matthew from Mark's eschatological discourse in Mark chapter 13, where, immediately before the Passion, Jesus is preparing his disciples for the future of the Church.

The persecution predicted is amply illustrated not only by the Acts of the Apostles, the Book of Revelation and Paul's account of his ministry in 2 Corinthians 11, but in every age of the Church up to the present time.

The 'councils' or 'sanhedrins' (Greek synedrion) do not refer to any formal legislative and judicial body at Jerusalem – it is very doubtful whether they existed at any time before the destruction of Jerusalem in 70 AD, still less the 'Great Sanhedrin' which claimed to rule Judaism in the second century. The term simply refers to a body of Jewish elders or officials anywhere. 'Sanhedrin' literally means 'a sitting together'. Similarly, 'synagogue' means primarily 'a gathering', and firm evidence for any building which could be called a synagogue is scanty in the first century.

Jerusalem, Jerusalem, the city that kills the prophets and stones those who are sent to it! How often have I desired to gather your children together as a hen gathers her brood under her wings, and you were not willing!

(Matthew 23:37)

It is often held that the lengthy time-perspective of these sayings is foreign to the mind of Jesus, who was wholly concentrated on the urgency of the completion of the kingship of God. However, even if the temporal perspective has changed, this is merely an application of such strong assertions, authenticated throughout the gospel tradition, of the union between Jesus and those who carry his word.

As verse 20 suggests, the early Christians were vividly aware of the Spirit at work in all aspects and activities of the community. This is clear from the letters of Paul, particularly in Galatians 3:1-3 and 1 Corinthians 12-14, from the Johannine discourses after the Last Supper (*John* 14-17), and from the accounts of the activity of the first community in Jerusalem (*Acts* 4:31 and 5:32).

See, I am sending you out like sheep into the midst of wolves; so be wise as serpents and innocent as doves.

(Matthew 10:16)

The Dogmatic Constitution on the Church from the Second Vatican Council reads:

The Spirit dwells in the Church and in the hearts of the faithful as in a temple. The Spirit guides the Church into the fulness of truth and gives her a unity of fellowship and service. By the power of the gospel he makes the Church grow, perpetually renews her and leads her to perfect union with her spouse

(Lumen Gentium 4).

The Word Lives on

The first section of these instructions for the mission of Jesus' disciples (from 9:36 to 10:8) is read on the Eleventh Sunday of Year A. Sections of the passage are also read from Tuesday to Friday during the fourteenth week of Ordinary Time.

Matthew 10:7-13 is the gospel reading for the Memorial of St Barnabas, while Matthew 10:17-22 can be chosen as the gospel reading for the memorials of martyrs. This latter reading is laid down to be read on the Feast of St Stephen, the first Christian martyr.

The Stoning of St Stephen by Giacinto Gimignani. St Stephen wears a dalmatic because he was held to be the first deacon.

Live the Word of God

Listen again to the reading: Matthew 9:36 - 10:20.

What do you hear now?
Suggestions for reflection and prayer

How does the persecution of Christians show itself in the present century? Do I invite persecution by my life as a Christian? Do I lessen my Christian commitment to avoid persecution?

- Pray for courage to put up with persecution for being Christian, in whatever form it comes.
- Pray that those who are seriously persecuted for their faith may have the courage to persevere.
- Pray to respect the faith of others, even if it is not Christian faith.

How does the activity of the Holy Spirit manifest itself in the church of today? Is the Church a prophetic community? How do I play my part in this community?

- Pray for a deeper understanding of the work of the Holy Spirit today in men and women who do the work of God.
- Pray for a greater alertness to the demands of the Spirit.
- Pray for an ever deeper understanding of the mysteries of faith.

What is the best way in which I can carry and live the gospel of Christ? Am I truly committed to living the gospel?

- Pray to understand and love the Good News of Jesus more whole-heartedly, and for the grace to attend to it more faithfully when it is read.
- Pray for an advance of the gospel in mission territories both at home and abroad, and for zeal and perseverance in those who work to spread the gospel.
- Pray for an insight into the ways in which I give scandal by my failures in living the gospel, and for greater fidelity to the demands of the gospel.

The Dogmatic Constitution on the Church from the Second Vatican Council reads:

The lay apostolate is a participation in the saving mission of the Church itself. Through their baptism all are commissioned to that apostolate by the Lord himself. The laity are called in a special way to make the Church present and operative in those places and circumstances where only through them can she become the salt of the earth.

(Lumen Gentium, 33).

Matthew's Parables

Hear the Word of God

Read: Matthew 13:24-43

[24] He put before them another parable: 'The kingdom of heaven may be compared to someone who sowed good seed in his field; [25] but while everybody was asleep, an enemy came and sowed weeds among the wheat, and then went away. [26] So when the plants came up and bore grain, then the weeds appeared as well. [27] And the slaves of the householder came and said to him, 'Master, did you not sow good seed in your field? Where, then, did these weeds come from?' [28] He answered, 'An enemy has done this.' The slaves said to him, 'Then do you want us to go and gather them?' [29] But he replied, 'No; for in gathering the weeds you would uproot the wheat along with them. [30] Let both of them grow together until the harvest; and at harvest time I will tell the reapers, Collect the weeds first and bind them in bundles to be burned, but gather the wheat into my barn.' '

[31] He put before them another parable: 'The kingdom of heaven is like a mustard seed that someone took and sowed in his field; [32] it is the smallest of all the seeds, but when it has grown it is the greatest of shrubs and becomes a tree, so that the birds of the air come and make nests in its branches.'

[33] He told them another parable: 'The kingdom of heaven is like yeast that a woman took and mixed in with three measures of flour until all of it was leavened.'

[34] Jesus told the crowds all these things in parables; without a parable he told them nothing. [35] This was to fulfil what had been spoken through the prophet: 'I will open my mouth to speak in parables; I will proclaim what has been hidden from the foundation of the world.'

[36] Then he left the crowds and went into the house. And his disciples approached him, saying, 'Explain to us the parable of the weeds of the field.' [37] He answered, 'The one who sows the good seed is the Son of Man; [38] the field is the world, and the good seed are the children of the kingdom; the weeds are the children of the evil one, [39] and the enemy who sowed them is the devil; the harvest is the end of the age, and the reapers are angels. [40] Just as the weeds are collected and burned up with fire, so will it be at the end of the age. [41] The Son of Man will send his angels, and they will collect out of his kingdom all causes of sin and all evildoers, [42] and they will throw them into the furnace of fire, where there will be weeping and gnashing of teeth. [43] Then the righteous will shine like the sun in the kingdom of their Father. Let anyone with ears listen!'

Opposite: The Parable of the Devil Sowing Tares while the Farmer Sleeps, Adriaen I van Nieulandt, (1587-1658).

Understand the Word of God

This session will explore:

- ❖ The purpose of parables
- ❖ Features of Matthew's parables
- ❖ Matthew's preoccupation with final judgment
- ❖ The use of proverbial wisdom in the gospels

Setting in the Gospel

Matthew follows Mark (chapter 4) in giving a collection of Jesus' parables after the early part of Jesus' ministry. This forms the central discourse of Matthew's five great discourses (see above on the Sermon on the Mount). Each discourse is about a different aspect of the Kingdom of God, which forms the principal object of his attention, and this central discourse gives images of the Kingdom. Like any good teacher – and especially a teacher who teaches by word of mouth – Jesus used images to fix the material in his hearers' minds.

In each of the collections, Mark's as well as Matthew's, the first parable is the Sower, which was probably originally Jesus' own reflection on the failure of most people to respond to his message, despite his trying every way of proclaiming it. By contrast, the little group of chosen disciples responded and bore great fruit.

Our passage, however, begins after that, and here Matthew deserts Mark. While Mark's seed parable is 'The Seed Growing Secretly', an image of the Kingdom growing in ways which human beings cannot fathom, Matthew's parable is that of the Seed and the Darnel, which is a warning. Matthew has a different message to emphasise. In the translation given above, from the New Revised Standard Version, the word 'darnel' is not used, but simply 'weeds'. The Greek word *zizania* used here by Matthew denotes a particular type of troublesome weed, which resembles wheat.

Matthew likes to give his parables in pairs. So here the parable of the Wheat and the Darnel is paired by the Drag-net (13:47-50), where the net, like the cornfield, contains good and bad as well, to be sorted out only at the end of time. Similarly, the Mustard-Seed and the Yeast form a pair: great results from paltry beginnings. Matthew will go on to give us another pair, the Pearl of Great Price and the Buried Treasure.

In Mark, the first gospel to be written, Jesus teaches urgently that the Kingdom of God has arrived and there is no time to lose. An immediate decision is necessary. You must change your ways now, for the Kingdom of God is upon you. In Matthew the emphasis is different. Matthew is vividly aware that the Church is the Kingdom of God, already at work in the world. A decision is still urgently necessary, but Matthew looks ahead to the end-time. The end, which the Markan Jesus is seen to be proclaiming so urgently, is not yet, but comes only after a period in which Jesus' disciples must live in the world according to the principles of morality which Jesus has declared. At the end they will be examined on these. And so at the end there are the great parables of the Ten Talents (how have you used the talents you were given?), of the Wedding-Feast (have you acquired for yourself a wedding garment, the traditional Jewish symbol of good works?), of the Wise and Foolish Wedding Attendants (have you prepared yourself with a good supply of oil?), of the Sheep and the Goats (have you treated the 'little ones' as you would treat Christ himself?). The final judgment-scene bulks large in Matthew's thinking and his message.

Contrast is also a recurrent feature of Matthew's parables, for Matthew is acutely aware that the world is divided into good and bad. Nearly all the parables that come in Matthew alone have this feature of contrast: the Wheat and the Darnel, the Playing Children (11:16-18), the Two Sons (21:28-32), the Two Debtors (18:23-35), as well as the final judgment-parables already mentioned. Matthew paints in primary colours: his characters are black and white, good or bad. He has no room for mixed motives, as can be seen in the characters in Luke's parables, who do the right things for the wrong reasons. The Prodigal Son returns home simply because he is hungry, and the Unjust Judge gives the widow her due simply to save his face.

Christ the Judge Separating the Sheep from the Goats, Church of Sant' Apollinare Nuovo, Ravenna.

What kind of text?

The parable of Nathan to David:

Nathan came to David (after his adultery with Bathsheba) and said: 'In the same town there were two men, one rich, the other poor. The rich man had flocks and herds in great abundance; the poor man had nothing but a ewe lamb, only a single little one which he had bought. He fostered it and it grew up with him and his children; it was like a daughter to him. When a traveller came to stay, the rich man would not take anything from his own flock or herd to provide for the wayfarer. Instead he stole the poor man's lamb and prepared that for his guest.' David flew into a great rage with the man: 'The man who did this deserves to die!' Nathan then said to David, 'You are the man.'

(2 Samuel 12:1-7)

All good teachers, as we have said, use images and stories to lodge their message in their hearers' minds. Of this kind are Aesop's Fables or the stories of Anthony de Mello. This practice was particularly strong in Israel's Wisdom tradition. The Old Testament contains large collections of such imaged sayings. The concept of *mashal* (plural *meshalim*) is not exactly proverb or parable or story or riddle. It includes all of these, and any wise or canny saying which includes an image or which needs reflection to bring out its depth. In the more developed Wisdom tradition we have whole collections of proverbs ('He takes a stray dog by the ears who meddles in someone else's quarrel', *Proverbs* 26:17. 'A fool laughs at the top of his voice, but the intelligent quietly smiles', *Sirach* 21:20). Sayings of this kind were known all over the Near East. 'Better is bread when the heart is happy than riches in sorrow' is found in the Egyptian sayings of Amen-em-Opet. Parables are particularly popular in rabbinic literature and in all the witty tradition of Jewish story-telling.

Each of the evangelists uses parables in his own particular way, for, although they were inspired, their own particular mind-set and personality moulds the way they express their message. Mark uses brief images of a homely kind (salt, wineskins, patches of cloth, a thief) to illustrate the nature of the Kingdom itself. He has only four or five longer, developed story-type parables. Matthew adds a clutch of longer contrast-stories about people fulfilling or not fulfilling the requirements for entry into the Kingdom, always with an eye upon future judgment. Luke gives more subtle examples of wisdom or folly, often enlivened by lively speech (the excuses of the invited guests who have other priorities, *Luke* 14:18-20), and illustrating his favourite themes of prayer and divine forgiveness. In John the only image approaching a story-parable is the Good Shepherd (*John* 10).

Commentary: verse by verse reading

The Wheat and the Darnel

vv. 24-30 The Parable of the Darnel is one of the most clearly allegorical of all the parables, that is, each element has its corresponding reality. This is not the case for all parables, for some of them have a single point of comparison, a single meaning to convey. When the Lord is said to come like a thief in the night or like the labour-pains of a pregnant woman, it does not necessarily mean that the Lord is dishonest or that his coming is painful, but only that it is unpredictably sudden. Both the Sower and the Darnel have keys provided (*Matthew* 13:19-23 and 36-43) in which each element of the story is de-coded.

Matthew likes allegories and tends to allegorise parables which were not necessarily originally intended as allegories. So he uses the Hired Vineyard Workers (20:1-16) to illustrate 'the first shall be last and the last first', when its original meaning was not the order of payment but the impossibility of calculating rewards with God.

In the Parable of the Darnel the allegory applies the story to the final judgment in a way quite characteristic of Matthew and in phrases beloved of him, the angels sent out into the world, the blazing furnace, weeping and grinding of teeth and 'the Kingdom of the Father'. It is possible to establish a striking list of words and phrases in the explanation which occur only in Matthew, so that one can only conclude that the explanation as we now have it was written by Matthew. In other words, Matthew sees the parable as illustrating the lesson so important for his own Judaeo-Christian community: you must work in faith for the Kingdom, since you will finally be judged on the criterion of these works.

St Augustine provides this interpretation:

Let the one who is wheat persevere until the harvest; let those who are weeds be changed into wheat. In the Lord's field, which is the Church, at times what was grain turns into weeds and at times what were weeds turn into grain, and no one knows what they will be tomorrow.

(Sermon 73)

From St Jerome:

We are advised not to be quick in cutting off a fellow-believer, for it may happen that one who has been corrupted today by evil may recover his senses tomorrow by sound teaching and abide by the truth.

(Commentary on Matthew 13:29-30)

Parables are, however, by their nature polyvalent. ('A stitch in time saves nine' has many applications.) It is always valuable to try to discern the circumstances in which Jesus might have told the story, not necessarily with the full allegorical apparatus or intention. Jesus could have spoken the parable to teach that there is good and bad in every person, rather than in every society, or at least in the Christian society. He could have been replying to a gibe about his encouraging sinners. For Matthew, however, the lesson is clear: even in the Church there are sinners. It is a Church of sinners, and we should not expect perfection, perhaps not even from the leaders of the Church.

The Mustard Seed

vv.31-32 The paired Parables of the Mustard-Seed and of the Leaven teach a wholly different lesson. The original circumstances for each of them could be as a reply either to Jesus' opponents or to his followers. In the former case he is replying to opponents who mock any pretensions to be renewing Israel through the choice of these twelve undistinguished peasants. In the latter case he is responding to the discouragement of his followers: 'how can we, wretched little group that we are, constitute the New Israel?' In both cases Jesus' reply is in fact 'Wait and see! Small beginnings can produce a great result'.

Mustard seeds are indeed tiny, and can easily be mistaken for mere dust. I have myself seen in Palestine a mustard-plant, bushy and some two metres tall, where there was none the previous year. Perhaps it is an exaggeration to call it a tree (though a little bird balanced delicately on one of its stems or branches), but this too has a point. In Daniel chapter 4 a tree represents a great empire with food for all in it, providing shade for the wild animals, with the birds of heaven nesting in its branches. Is the mustard-tree then a hint that all the nations of the world will find shelter in the Christian community?

From the Commentary of Saint Hilary:

The Lord compared his reign with a grain of mustard-seed, which is very pungent and the smallest of all seeds. Its inherent potency is enhanced under stress and pressure. Therefore, after this grain is sown in the field it grows up to become larger than any herb and surpasses all the glory of the prophets.

(On Matthew 13.4)

The Leaven

v.33 The lesson of the Leaven is slightly different. The paradox here is that a tiny pinch of yeast can leaven a huge mound of dough. The Greek translated 'three measures' indicates some 25 kg of dough, enough for several dozen people. Perhaps Jesus is teaching the extraordinary effect on the world that a small and unimpressive group of people can have – especially since leaven was itself considered a corrupt substance, to be thrown out for the cleanliness of the new harvest. Alternatively, he may be stressing the abundance of the messianic plenty, as in the story of the immense amount of wine which Jesus offered at the Marriage Feast of Cana (*John* 2:1-12).

From St John Chrysostom:

The leaven, though it is buried, is not destroyed. Little by little it transmutes the whole lump into its own condition. This happens with the gospel. Do not fear, then, that there will be many dangerous circumstances. For even then you will shine forth and be victorious.

(Homily 46.2)

The Word Lives on

The whole of this passage, containing the parables of the Darnel, the Mustard-Seed and the Yeast, is provided in the lectionary to be read on the Sixteenth Ordinary Sunday of Year A. In the weekday lectionary the passage is read on Saturday of the sixteenth week of Ordinary Time, and continued on Monday and Tuesday of the seventeenth week.

Live the Word of God

Listen again to the reading: Matthew 13:24-43

What do you hear now?

Suggestions for reflection and prayer

Am I judgmental, deciding who is the 'darnel' in the church and writing them off? Or do I try to understand their difficulties and help them to a better path? In what respects am I myself 'darnel'? In what ways will I need to be purified when it comes to the Judgment, so that I can face the awesome glory of God?

> ❖Pray for a greater awareness of your own faults and hypocrisies.
> ❖ Pray for the grace to make a real effort to reform.
> ❖ Pray for those who are lost on the way to the Lord, that they may find their way and stick to it.

If I was in that little group of Jesus' twelve disciples would I really live the confidence that we were establishing the Kingdom of God on earth? Anyway, do I play my part now? What can I think of recently that I have done that has brought peace and healing and obedience to God's love a little closer? What have I done recently to impede the Kingdom?

> ❖Pray for all those who have a special task in manifesting the Kingship of God, bishops, priests, all kinds of ministers, all those who exercise the ministry of healing, teaching, motherhood, fatherhood in the Church.
> ❖ Pray for the strength to heal any wounds you may have inflicted.
> ❖ Pray especially for forgiveness and the grace to forgive others.

Am I growing like the mustard-plant in the Kingdom of God, leavening by my love those with whom I come in contact, or am I shrinking and withering, souring the efforts of those who try to live as Christians?

> ❖ Pray to be leaven in the Kingdom of God.
> ❖ Pray for those who are losing heart.
> ❖ Pray for those who have not yet come in contact with the leaven.
> ❖ Pray that the mustard seed may be growing and bearing fruit in your own community.

From the Catechism of the Catholic Church:

Jesus' invitation to enter his kingdom comes in the form of parables, a characteristic feature of his teaching. Through his parables he invites people to the feast of the kingdom, but he also asks for a radical choice: to gain the kingdom, one must give everything. (546)

Peter's Profession of Faith
and its sequels

Hear the Word of God

Read: Matthew 16:13-28

[13] Now when Jesus came into the district of Caesarea Philippi, he asked his disciples, 'Who do people say that the Son of Man is?' [14] And they said, 'Some say John the Baptist, but others Elijah, and still others Jeremiah or one of the prophets.' [15] He said to them, 'But who do you say that I am?' [16] Simon Peter answered, 'You are the Messiah, the Son of the living God.' [17] And Jesus answered him, 'Blessed are you, Simon son of Jonah! For flesh and blood has not revealed this to you, but my Father in heaven. [18] And I tell you, you are Peter, and on this rock I will build my church, and the gates of Hades will not prevail against it. [19] I will give you the keys of the kingdom of heaven, and whatever you bind on earth will be bound in heaven, and whatever you loose on earth will be loosed in heaven.' [20] Then he sternly ordered the disciples not to tell anyone that he was the Messiah.

[21] From that time on, Jesus began to show his disciples that he must go to Jerusalem and undergo great suffering at the hands of the elders and chief priests and scribes, and be killed, and on the third day be raised. [22] And Peter took him aside and began to rebuke him, saying, 'God forbid it, Lord! This must never happen to you.' [23] But he turned and said to Peter, 'Get behind me, Satan! You are a stumbling-block to me; for you are setting your mind not on divine things but on human things.'

[24] Then Jesus told his disciples, 'If any want to become my followers, let them deny themselves and take up their cross and follow me. [25] For those who want to save their life will lose it, and those who lose their life for my sake will find it. [26] For what will it profit them if they gain the whole world but forfeit their life? Or what will they give in return for their life?

[27] 'For the Son of Man is to come with his angels in the glory of his Father, and then he will repay everyone for what has been done. [28] Truly I tell you, there are some standing here who will not taste death before they see the Son of Man coming in his kingdom.'

Opposite: Caesarea Philippi (Banias) by Harry Fenn, (1845–1911).

Understand the Word of God

This session will explore:

- ❖ The naming and commissioning of Peter
- ❖ The presence of Christ in the Church
- ❖ The difficulty of grasping the message of the cross
- ❖ The moment of the coming of the Kingdom

Setting in the Gospel

It is quite difficult to explain the setting in the gospel of this passage. The corresponding passage in Mark chapter 8 is the turning-point of his gospel: the first part of the gospel has painted the scene of the disciples slowly, Oh so slowly, coming to understand that Jesus is the Messiah. Suddenly, after the healing of the blind man at Bethsaida, Peter's eyes are opened and he declares that Jesus is the Messiah. But immediately he shows that he still does not understand. When Jesus begins to reveal that he is to be a suffering Messiah (the theme of the second half of the gospel), Peter dismisses the idea out of hand, and is heavily rebuked.

Matthew does not seem to have perceived this pattern. He mitigates the slowness of the disciples, and indeed Peter has already, together with the other disciples, declared Jesus to be not only Messiah but son of God (14:33). Matthew's pattern, in five books, has now reached the fourth book, about the training of the disciples, and this passage falls between the parable-discourse (chapter 13) and the community-discourse (chapter 18). Accordingly, for Matthew, with his eye always firmly fixed on the community which is the Church, the significance of this passage is wholly other than its significance in Mark. It is the foundation-text of the Church, the New Israel, to which Jesus gives authority to bring his presence to the world. For this reason Matthew makes significant additions to the Markan text.

What kind of text?

Apart from the significant difference of Peter now acknowledging Jesus as both Messiah and 'son of the living God', the chief difference from Mark is the insertion in verses 17-19 of a series of promises. This makes it a commissioning text, not unlike the final commission by the Risen Christ on the mountain in Galilee, with which the gospel ends. But where did Matthew get this material, which is not in Mark? There are strong indications that a Semitic, possibly Aramaic, text lies behind it, though it is marked also by Matthew's own style and theology.

Each of the gospels, except Mark, contains some sort of commission to Peter, couched in various ways. Luke gathers several important sayings about the future situation of the Church, and puts them as a farewell speech of Jesus at the Last Supper in chapter 22. He includes there the word of comfort to Peter: 'Simon, Simon, listen! Satan has demanded to sift all of you like wheat, but I have prayed for you that your own faith may not fail; and you, when once you have turned back, strengthen your brothers.' (*Luke* 22:31-32)

John puts a similar promise in the scene at the lakeside in Galilee, when the Risen Christ three times tests out Peter's love, and three times charges him, 'Feed my sheep' (*John* 21:15-17). It is possible that each of the evangelists is reflecting in his own way the oral tradition of Jesus entrusting authority to the community he leaves behind him, and especially to Peter at its head.

The final commission by the Risen Christ:

Jesus came and said to them, 'All authority in heaven and on earth has been given to me. Go therefore and make disciples of all nations, baptising them in the name of the Father and of the Son and of the Holy Spirit, and teaching them to obey everything that I have commanded you.

(Matthew 28:18-20)

Statue in St Peter's Square

Commentary: verse by verse reading

Peter's Profession of Jesus as the Christ

v.13 Caesarea Philippi is in the far north of Galilee, at the foot of the mighty, snow-covered Mount Hermon, now just on the border of Syria. Its higher climate is much less sultry than that of the lake-towns, Capernaum and Bethsaida, where Jesus centred his ministry. It served as a relaxation point for the Roman soldiery when they later took control of Galilee. Did Jesus take the disciples there on a sort of group-retreat, to make this event particularly special?

In Matthew's version (not in Mark's) Jesus uses of himself the special phrase 'son of man'. This mysterious Aramaic expression is used in the New Testament only by Jesus, and was obviously a 'trade-mark' of his speech, treasured by his followers. In itself it means no more than 'human being'. It seems to have been used at that time as a sort of self-effacing identifier, much like the English 'one' ('one sometimes finds oneself in awkward situations'), particularly to avoid boasting or shocking.

I saw one like a son of man coming with the clouds of heaven, and he came to the Ancient One. To him was given dominion and glory and kingship, that all peoples, nations and languages should serve him (Daniel 7:13-14).

So Jesus uses it of his claims to divine authority (*Matthew* 9:6 and 12:8) and in the prophecies of the Passion. To Christians it has also the powerful overtones of the Son of Man in Daniel's vision, to whom all power is given.

v.14 The puzzled disciples have got as far as realising that Jesus had broken the long silence during which there had been no prophet in Israel. It is clear from the Jewish historian Josephus, as well as from the gospel (*Matthew* 21:25-26), that John the Baptist had been a well-known and respected figure, perhaps more prominent in the popular mind than Jesus himself. Josephus says that Herod Antipas feared that he would spark a messianic revolt.

Herod feared that the great influence John had over the people might incline him to raise a rebellion, for they seemed ready to do anything he advised. So he thought it best by putting him to death to prevent any mischief he might cause.

(Josephus, Antiquities 18.5)

vv.15-16 It was Peter, however, who affirmed that Jesus was not only the Messiah but also the son of God. In Matthew 14:33 the disciples had already declared this, though in Mark the centurion at the foot of the Cross is the first human being to acknowledge Jesus as such. Historically neither the centurion nor the disciples necessarily meant 'Son of God' in the sense taught by John ('The Word became flesh'). 'Son of God' is used in the Old Testament of angels (*Job* 1:6), of Israel itself (*Hosea* 11:1-4) and of the just man (*Wisdom* 2:13, 18). The way is, however, open to the full explanation given by John as 'equal to the Father'.

Job 1:6 One day the sons of God came to present themselves before the Lord.

Hosea 11:1 When Israel was a child, I loved him, and out of Egypt I called my son.

Wisdom 2:13 He professes to have knowledge of God, and calls himself a child of the Lord.

Wisdom 2:18 For if the righteous man is God's son, he will help him.

Giving of the Keys to St. Peter, from the Sistine Chape by Pietro Perugino, Vatican City, Italy.

- 73 -

Peter's Commission

v.17 Now begins the commissioning which occurs only in Matthew. Phrases with an Aramaic ring abound, suggesting that it is based on ancient material handed down orally: the beatitude 'blessed are you' reminiscent of the Psalms, the Hebrew name 'Simon' and the Aramaic 'Bar (=son of) Jonah', and the biblical pair 'flesh and blood'. On the other hand 'my Father in heaven' is a favourite phrase of Matthew, used seventeen times in the gospel.

v.18 Jesus now replies to Simon's acknowledgement of who he is by giving Simon himself the new name 'Peter'. This is the Greek word, meaning 'Rock', but the Aramaic name with the same meaning ('*Kepha*') occurs in John 1:42. Paul, writing some 20 years after the Resurrection, far earlier than Matthew, uses this name eight times, and only once the Greek translation 'Peter'. We can only guess why Jesus gave Simon this nickname. Was it because of his physical build, or his stubbornness or because of his function in the Church?

The most crucial element of all is 'on this Rock I will build my Church'. The word 'Church' (*ekklesia*) is used in the gospels only here and at 18:17. This alone shows how central to Matthew's message it is that Jesus is here founding an ecclesial community. The word is used in the Greek translation of the Old Testament to render *qahal*, the Hebrew word which means the gathering of God. Now Jesus' *qahal* is the successor to God's *qahal* in the Old Testament. It is the new People of God.

Epiphanius writes:

Christ is a rock which is never disturbed or worn away. Therefore Peter gladly received his name from Christ to signify the established and unshaken faith of the Church. The faith of the apostle, which was founded upon the rock of Christ, abides unconquered and unshaken.

(PL 3.869)

Matthew stresses that the *ekklesia* of Jesus is given its character by the divine presence of the Risen Lord. So in 1:23 at the beginning of the gospel Jesus is called significantly 'Emmanuel', which means 'God is with us'. The gospel is similarly 'book-ended' by the promise of the Risen Christ, 'I am with you always, to the end of the age' (28:20). Then in the middle we are told, 'Where two or three are gathered in my name, I am there among them' (18:20). This is the basis of the divine authority of the Church.

v.19 Now the authority is given to Peter. The imagery of the keys is obvious enough, as is shown by the gift of front-door keys to an 18-year-old, as his/her own, no longer simply a practical arrangement. There is no need to quote Old Testament parallels! Binding and loosing is another example of Hebrew style: the two opposites include everything in between, from one extreme to the other. It means that all the decisions taken by Peter have the divine authority and validity imparted by the presence of Christ in his Church. The contrast 'heaven' and 'earth' is a way of saying that the decisions and guidance have real and permanent validity.

Most important, however, is the gift of the same authority to the Church as a whole in 18:18, which reads: 'Truly, I tell you, whatever you bind on earth will be bound in heaven, and whatever you loose on earth will be loosed in heaven.' Peter is given in his own person the authority which the Church has. It is the community in which Christ is present that is primary, and the individual only secondary. The Second Vatican Council expressed this by saying that the community of the Church is itself a kingly, priestly and prophetic people.

v.20 The revelation is incomplete. Peter has understood that Jesus is the Messiah and son of God. But the disciples are forbidden to proclaim this until they have understood what this means. Very soon, after the Transfiguration (17:9), they will be told that the moment for releasing the news is after the Resurrection.

Jesus declares on three occasions that he is to suffer and die before rising again. Not surprisingly the disciples remain puzzled, for the concept of a Messiah (let alone a son of God) who would suffer and die is so paradoxical to Judaism as to be almost unintelligible. It makes sense only when the loving obedience of the Messiah and son to his Father has overturned the disobedience of Adam, and when the Father has vindicated the Son by raising him from death. Only then could they see how the Messiah, God's glorious representative on earth, could accept this role. It is only when these events have actually occurred that the Holy Spirit gives them the light to understand.

Jesus Christ is the one whom the Father anointed with the Holy Spirit and established as priest, prophet and king. The whole People of God participates in these three offices of Christ and bears the responsibilities for mission and service that flow from them.

(Catechism of the Catholic Church 783)

The First Prophecy of the Passion

vv. 21-23 Jesus gives three major, formal prophecies of his Passion and Resurrection (16:21, 17:22-23 and 20:17-19). Each time the disciples misunderstand. Mark, from whom Matthew derives this pattern, frequently uses triplets to stress a point, as with Jesus' three prayers at Gethsemane and Peter's three denials. Here, on this first occasion, Jesus' rebuke to Peter is particularly severe, but then Peter's rejection of the idea of Jesus suffering was also pretty rough. In Mark Peter is fairly mild, he 'began to rebuke him'. In Matthew, despite calling Jesus 'Lord', Peter's speech would be more fairly translated, 'May God forgive you, Lord. This shall not be.'

Matthew also strengthens Jesus' reply, by adding 'You are a stumbling-block to me'. Matthew is clearly making a point about Peter. As in the scene of the Walking on the Water, he begins well but then loses it (14:30). The same happens at the high priest's house. He has the courage to go that far, but what a mess he makes when he gets there!

Each of the three formal prophecies of the Passion is misunderstood by the disciples. After the second we find the disciples blandly squabbling about who is the greatest, and after the third the sons of Zebedee merely ask brazenly for the best seats in the kingdom.

vv.24-26 The saying about the cross occurs in all the gospels in many different forms, with the slightest of variations. It was one of the best remembered of Jesus' sayings.

It is worth noting that in the Aramaic original of these sayings it is not just a question of losing one's life. In Aramaic 'life' can be used for 'self', so that Jesus is talking about self-destruction if one fails to be whole-hearted in discipleship.

vv.27-28 This series of sayings ends with Matthew's typical emphasis on judgment, in the language of the Last Judgment parable (25:31).

From St John Chrysostom:

Note that he does not say, 'You must suffer whether you will it or not.' Rather he says, ' If anyone will come after me, let him deny himself and take up his cross and follow me.' That is to say, 'I force no one. I compel no one, but each one I make master of his own choice. So I say: If anyone will.'

(Homily 55.1)

We also come face-to-face with Jesus' expectation of the coming of the Kingdom. Was he wrong that 'some standing here' would see the coming of the Kingdom in power? The earliest Christians, with their Aramaic prayer 'Come, Lord Jesus' (1 *Corinthians* 16:22 and *Revelation* 22:20), were certainly expecting a speedy return of the Lord. Or does this saying refer to the awesome demonstration of the Kingdom at the Transfiguration which immediately follows this verse?

Perhaps we should say that the Kingdom comes in different ways at different times and that at the last supper (26:29) and at the trial (26:64) Jesus is referring to the definitive establishment of the Kingdom at his death and resurrection.

26:29 I tell you, I will never again drink of this fruit of the vine, until that day when I drink it new with you in my Father's kingdom.

26:64 From now on you will see the Son of Man seated at the right hand of Power and coming on the clouds of heaven.

The Word Lives on

This section of the Gospel of Matthew is read regularly on the 21st and 22nd Sundays in Ordinary Time in Year A. In the weekday lectionary the passage is read on Thursday and Friday of Week 18 each year.

Matthew 16:13-19 is, not surprisingly, read on the Solemnity of Saints Peter and Paul and on the Feast of the Chair of Peter, and is one of the alternative gospels offered for the feasts of Pastors. Matthew 16:24-27 is an alternative gospel reading for the memorials of saints, and for the sacraments of baptism and confirmation.

The Crucifixion of St. Peter, 1600-01 by Caravaggio, Santa Maria del Popolo, Rome.

Live the Word of God

Listen again to the reading: Matthew 16:13-28

What do you hear now?

Suggestions for reflection and prayer

Do I in any serious way set about discovering more about Jesus by prayer and reading? Do I attend to the readings at Mass? Do I thirst to discover more about my faith?

- ❖ Pray for zeal in deepening your faith.
- ❖ Pray that the Church may always be faithful to her Lord.
- ❖ Pray for pastors who will teach vibrantly about the Lord.

Do I take up my cross and follow Jesus? Or do I whimp out at anything that costs? Or complain miserably at any pain I can't avoid?

- ❖ Pray for the strength to face hard decisions for Jesus' sake
- ❖ Pray for the courage to accept physical pain and to join it to the cross of Jesus.
- ❖ Pray for the discernment to see suffering as Christ's gift.

What do I mean when I pray 'Thy kingdom come!'? Do I really want it to come? Wouldn't it rather upset me and cramp my style? Am I doing anything to bring it nearer realisation in the world around me?

- ❖ Pray earnestly for the wisdom to further Christ's Kingdom.
- ❖ Pray for the objectivity to see where Christ's Kingdom lies.
- ❖ Pray not to be a stumbling-block to others.

The Pastoral Constitution on the Church in the Modern World of the Second Vatican Council reads:

By suffering for us Jesus not only gave us an example so that we might follow in his footsteps, but he also opened up a way. If we follow this path, life and death are made holy and acquire a new meaning.

(Gaudium et Spes 22)

The Community Discourse

Hear the Word of God

Read: Matthew 18:1-20

18[1] At that time the disciples came to Jesus and asked, 'Who is the greatest in the kingdom of heaven?' [2] He called a child, whom he put among them, [3] and said, 'Truly I tell you, unless you change and become like children, you will never enter the kingdom of heaven. [4] Whoever becomes humble like this child is the greatest in the kingdom of heaven. [5] Whoever welcomes one such child in my name welcomes me.

[6] 'If any of you put a stumbling-block before one of these little ones who believe in me, it would be better for you if a great millstone were fastened around your neck and you were drowned in the depth of the sea. [7] Woe to the world because of stumbling-blocks! Occasions for stumbling are bound to come, but woe to the one by whom the stumbling-block comes!

[8] 'If your hand or your foot causes you to stumble, cut it off and throw it away; it is better for you to enter life maimed or lame than to have two hands or two feet and to be thrown into the eternal fire. [9] And if your eye causes you to stumble, tear it out and throw it away; it is better for you to enter life with one eye than to have two eyes and to be thrown into the hell of fire.

[10] 'Take care that you do not despise one of these little ones; for, I tell you, in heaven their angels continually see the face of my Father in heaven. [12] What do you think? If a shepherd has a hundred sheep, and one of them has gone astray, does he not leave the ninety-nine on the mountains and go in search of the one that went astray? [13] And if he finds it, truly I tell you, he rejoices over it more than over the ninety-nine that never went astray. [14] So it is not the will of your Father in heaven that one of these little ones should be lost.

[15] 'If another member of the church sins against you, go and point out the fault when the two of you are alone. If the member listens to you, you have regained that one. [16] But if you are not listened to, take one or two others along with you, so that every word may be confirmed by the evidence of two or three witnesses. [17] If the member refuses to listen to them, tell it to the church; and if the offender refuses to listen even to the church, let such a one be to you as a Gentile and a tax-collector. [18] Truly I tell you, whatever you bind on earth will be bound in heaven, and whatever you loose on earth will be loosed in heaven. [19] Again, truly I tell you, if two of you agree on earth about anything you ask, it will be done for you by my Father in heaven. [20] For where two or three are gathered in my name, I am there among them.'

Opposite: Jesus Teaching, Artist unknown.

Understand the Word of God

This session will explore:

- ❖ the authority of the Christian community
- ❖ ranking within the Church
- ❖ reconciliation in the community
- ❖ the presence of Christ in his community

Setting in the Gospel

As was pointed out in the section on the Sermon on the Mount, Matthew's five great discourses of Jesus, or collections of his sayings, are arranged symmetrically, in a chiasmus. This fourth discourse on internal relationships within the community balances the second discourse (chapter 10) on the external mission of the community. It presents many aspects of what sort of person the member of the Christian community should be, and how members should relate to one another, setting a lofty ideal.

What kind of text?

This chapter could be called a legislative text, if there are such texts within Christianity. Pope Benedict teaches that Jesus came to show us the face of God in human form, and this vision of God should shape humanity in a way which would enable human beings to make their own judgments. Jesus has not left us a legislative text which covers every aspect of life, but this sketch of community relationships is an important formative factor. Some of the sayings here collected show Jesus' own originality. Others may have been taken over by him from traditional wisdom, as is suggested by the similarity with texts from Qumran. Still others will be Matthew's development and application of the teaching of Jesus.

Concrete juridical and social forms and political arrangements are no longer treated as a sacred law that is fixed for all times and so for all peoples. The decisive thing is the underlying communion of will with God given by Jesus.

(Benedict XVI, Jesus of Nazareth, p. 118).

Commentary: verse by verse reading

Rankings in the Community

vv.1-5 Immediately before this verse comes the second formal prophecy of the passion. Again the disciples show their failure to understand by immediately asking who the greatest is in the kingdom. No! This is not the question to ask! Jesus replies by an acted parable, taking a child as an example. The point of this example can easily be misunderstood. Is Jesus' point the innocence of children? Children can be as cunning and devious as any adult! Is it the receptivity and dependence of children? Children are used to receiving, and expect to do so. Christians must certainly be receptive and realise their dependence on their heavenly Father. Is it the teachability of children? Children are used to being taught and corrected. Christians must also be always ready to learn, an openness which becomes more difficult with age.

One significant factor is lack of status. In a more primitive, patriarchal society, where age and ancestry were much valued, and where infant mortality was disastrously high, children were not well protected, but were significantly lacking in status. At all events even adult Christians must change their way of life and scale of values. The Greek word used by Matthew means 'turn' (translated 'change'). This involves 'an about-turn': I am going in one direction, turn about and go in a totally different direction. This is the change of values required of the Christian.

The first quality which Jesus mentions is becoming humble, which fits the squabble about status which sparked his action in the first place. It also fits the third beatitude about the meek in Matthew 5:5, and Jesus' teaching in Matthew 11:29, 'Learn from me, for I am gentle and humble in heart.' His entry into Jerusalem as the humble king in 21:1-5 eschews all pomp and ceremony, and is stressed by Matthew as the fulfilment of scripture.

St Jerome comments as follows:

A child does not long remember injury suffered, is not passionately attracted by a beautiful woman, does not think one thing and say another. So you too, unless you have similar innocence and purity of mind, will not be able to enter the kingdom of heaven.

(On Matthew 3.18)

You are not to be called rabbis, for you are all brothers and sisters. And call no one your father on earth, for you have one Father – the one in heaven. Nor are you to be called instructors, for you have one instructor, the Messiah.

(Matthew 23:8-10).

Matthew reverts to the subject of rank in 23:8-11. In rabbinic teaching it was customary to put forward teaching in the name of particular rabbis or teachers: Rabbi X says this, Rabbi Y says that, Rabbi Z says the other. It is remarkable that there is no trace of such a process in the gospels: the only authority is Jesus himself. No instance or ruling is quoted on the authority of any other teacher. So Matthew reiterates the equality of all followers of Christ.

'These Little Ones'

vv.6-7 Reference to 'these little ones' comes in verses 6 and 10. There is also a further link with 'these little ones' in verse 14. However, the key-word here is 'stumbling-block', and the section is really a series of separate sayings collected and linked together by this idea, the idea of a rock which trips people up and causes them to fall over.

Who then are 'these little ones'? Traditionally, they have been regarded as the children made examples in the previous section. There is also an obvious link to the scene of the Last Judgment

(*Matthew* 25:35-42), where giving a drink to those in need is one of the criteria for being called to Jesus' right hand. On the other hand, it has been suggested that 'these little ones' who should be given a cup of water 'in the name of a disciple' (10:42) are more precisely Christian missioners – and of course all Christians are missioners - charged to spread the gospel. 'These little ones' would then be a technical term for the flock of Christ.

Other hints, however, such as the stumbling-block in verse 7, do seem to suggest that the little ones are more vulnerable than missioners would be. We may take the 'little ones' to be the vulnerable members of the community. In this case, one important element of 'becoming like children' is to be sensitive enough to be vulnerable, rather than brazen and self-sufficient.

Amputation?

St John Chrysostom comments:

He is not saying this about human limbs, but about friends and relatives whom we regard in the rank of necessary limbs. For nothing is so harmful as bad company. So he orders us with great emphasis to cut off those who are harmful to us, implying that these are people who supply temptations to sin.

(Homily on the Gospel of Matthew 59.4)

vv.8-9 Two hard sayings of Jesus follow. Shorter versions of these sayings have already been given in Matthew 5:29-30 in the Sermon on the Mount, in the context of adultery, where Matthew is gathering together sayings of Jesus to show how his teaching surpasses that of the Old Law. How should they be interpreted? It is well known that the great third-century scholar Origen is said to have taken the instructions literally and castrated himself to avoid sexual temptations. This may be part of the reason why he was never canonised as a model for all Christians.

Self-mutilation has never been part of the tradition of the Church. Does this mean that the Church has defected from its master's teaching? This is a real case where the traditional interpretation of the Church is vital in understanding Jesus' intention. It is always dangerous to take a single sentence in isolation from the wider teaching.

As the quotation from Benedict XVI above confirms, Jesus came not to promulgate a rule-book but to show the face of God. That being said, one must always have a reverent terror of relativising the absolute demands of Jesus.

The Sheep gone Astray

vv.10-14 There is a subtle difference between the telling of this parable in Matthew 18:10-14 and in Luke 15:4-7, attention to which helps to bring out both meanings. In Luke's version the sheep is lost, and the story ends with a double mention of repentance in 15:7. One of Luke's major thrusts, both in the gospel and in the Book of the Acts, is always encouraging conversion and repentance. Here he focuses on the joy in heaven at the repentance of one sinner.

In Matthew, on the other hand, the parable is all about going in search of a sheep which has gone astray. The context of the chapter on community relations also emphasises that the lesson taught is not joy at the repentance of a sinner, but the duty of a shepherd to go in search of the stray, and the joy of the successful shepherd. One might well ask whether a careful shepherd would indeed leave 99% of his sheep untended in order to search for the remaining one. However, even if this is not good shepherding, the exaggeration brings out still more the eagerness of the shepherd to recover the stray.

Reconciliation

vv.15-17 Matthew is no starry-eyed idealist. He knows well that in any community hurts and grudges will arise, that members of the community will upset one another. The important thing is reconciliation. So in 6:14-15, at the end of the Lord's Prayer, the petition he stresses is the one about mutual forgiveness: 'For if you forgive others their trespasses, your heavenly Father will also forgive you; but if you do not forgive others, neither will your Father forgive your trespasses.'

From the Catechism of the Catholic Church:

It is not in our power not to feel, or to forget, an offence; but the heart that offers itself to the Holy Spirit turns injury into compassion and purifies the memory in transforming the hurt into intercession. (n. 605)

In the same way, he devotes almost half this chapter on relationships within the community to the tricky matter of forgiveness, and concludes it with the fierce parable about the servant who was forgiven a simply immense debt, and refused to forgive his fellow-servant a paltry sum (18:23-35).

The process of reconciliation which Matthew prescribes is exactly similar to that prescribed in the Community Rule of Qumran. The offender must be confronted face to face. Witnesses are to be brought. The matter is then to be brought before the assembly. The Qumran Rule specifically forbids consideration in the assembly of any complaint which has not gone through the two previous stages.

They shall rebuke one another in truth, humility and charity. Let no one address a companion with anger or ill-temper. Let him not hate him, but let him rebuke him the very same day lest he incur guilt because of him. And furthermore, let no one accuse a companion before the Congregation without having admonished him in the presence of witnesses.

(Qumran Community Rule, 1QS 5-6).

Christ's Presence in the Community

vv.18-20 The final three verses before the parable of the servant, which concludes the discourse in verses 23-35, again establish the authority of the community. First is repeated the promise about binding and loosing, made at Caesarea Philippi in Matthew 16:19 to Peter individually as the rock on which the Church is built. The authority which Peter enjoys, therefore, is the authority given to the Church itself. Finally, the assurance is given that even the smallest gathering of the Church has this authority, and the reason for this is the presence of Christ in his community.

How seriously should 'in my name' be taken? This may be read as a warning that not every gathering of Christians is automatically in the name of Christ. This phrase occurs often enough in the New Testament. We are baptised into the name of Christ. We are those over whom the name of Christ is invoked. The name stands for the power of somebody. To be gathered in the power and the name of Christ means that certain conditions must be observed, not merely the Christian purpose of the gathering, but the conduct of the gathering too. Perhaps ideally the name of Christ should be explicit.

The Qumran scrolls also consider the community rather than the Jerusalem Temple to be the true Temple, the place where God dwells. This attitude is very similar to Matthew's teaching about the divine presence of Jesus in the Christian community as suggested in verse 20. It would be fascinating to speculate on the link between Matthew and the community of the scrolls. Did one learn from the other, and in this case which from which? Are both dependent on a teaching and practice which was common at the time? Since the value of the Qumran Scrolls is that they are the only religious documents from Palestine at the time of Jesus, the question remains unanswerable.

From Saint Cyril of Alexandria:

Even if only two harmoniously and deliberately define their requests, they will come to their goal. For it is not the number of those gathered but the strength of their piety and their love of God that is effective.

(Fragment 215)

Jesus and the twelve disciples. From the Four Gospels, in Slavonic, c.1355-c.1356.

The Word Lives on

On the 23rd Sunday in Ordinary Time in Year A Matthew 18:15-20 is read. Parts of Matthew 18:1-20 are also read on Tuesday and Wednesday of week 19 in the weekday lectionary.

On the second Tuesday of Advent the parable about finding the lost sheep helps prepare for the birth of the shepherd who comes to search out the lost. On the feast of the Guardian Angels the reading from Matthew 18 includes verse 10, where the angels of 'these little ones' continually see the face of the Father in heaven.

Parable of the lost sheep from 'Le Miroir de l'Humaine Salvation',Flemish School, (15th century).

Live the Word of God

Listen again to the reading: Matthew 18:1-20

What do you hear now?
Suggestions for reflection and prayer

Am I an influence for good, giving to those who meet me a vision of the honesty, joy and justice of Christ, or am I a stumbling-block, conniving at evil, encouraging crookedness, deception and injustice?

Am I respectful of other people with whom I deal? Do I think of their advantage as much as of my own? Or do I thoughtlessly kick them into corners or callously leave them to sink or swim?

Do I do enough for those who are incapable of helping themselves, either physically, emotionally or psychologically? Do I see in them the face of Christ suffering?

Do I do my part – whatever that may be – in taking a stand against the major injustices of world affairs? Am I courageous in speaking my mind against injustice?

❖ Pray for those who control world affairs by government, that they may be courageous and far-sighted in their policies, giving due prominence to unfortunate or hampered individuals and to whole countries in need of help.

❖ Pray for financiers and economists, that they may evolve practices which help those in need, that they may be honest and genuine.

❖ Pray for the 'little ones', the vulnerable, the injured, the long-term sick, those suffering family traumas, children suffering from their parents, parents suffering from their children.

❖ Pray to see the presence of Christ in his Church, despite its many shadows, and to play a part in spreading the light of Christ through the Church.

Christ is always present in his Church, especially in her liturgical celebrations. He is present in the sacrifice of the Mass, not only in the person of his minister, but especially in the Eucharistic species. By his power he is present in the sacraments, so that when anybody baptises it is really Christ himself who baptises. He is present in his word since it is he himself who speaks.

(Catechism of the Catholic Church, n. 1088)

Parable of the Labourers in the Vineyard

Hear the Word of God

Read: Matthew 20:1-16

20 [1] For the kingdom of heaven is like a landowner who went out early in the morning to hire labourers for his vineyard. [2] After agreeing with the labourers for the usual daily wage, he sent them into his vineyard. [3] When he went out about nine o'clock, he saw others standing idle in the market-place; [4] and he said to them, 'You also go into the vineyard, and I will pay you whatever is right.' So they went. [5] When he went out again about noon and about three o'clock, he did the same. [6] And about five o'clock he went out and found others standing around; and he said to them, 'Why are you standing here idle all day?' [7] They said to him, 'Because no one has hired us.' He said to them, 'You also go into the vineyard.' [8] When evening came, the owner of the vineyard said to his manager, 'Call the labourers and give them their pay, beginning with the last and then going to the first.' [9] When those hired about five o'clock came, each of them received the usual daily wage. [10] Now when the first came, they thought they would receive more; but each of them also received the usual daily wage. [11] And when they received it, they grumbled against the landowner, [12] saying, 'These last worked only one hour, and you have made them equal to us who have borne the burden of the day and the scorching heat.' [13] But he replied to one of them, 'Friend, I am doing you no wrong; did you not agree with me for the usual daily wage? [14] Take what belongs to you and go; I choose to give to this last the same as I give to you. [15] Am I not allowed to do what I choose with what belongs to me? Or are you envious because I am generous?' [16] So the last will be first, and the first will be last.

Opposite: Parable of the Labourers in the Vineyard 1637, by Rembrandt Harmensz van Rijn (1606-1669).

Understand the Word of God

This session will explore:

- ❖ Hypocrisy – Christian and Pharisaic
- ❖ Can you bargain with God?
- ❖ Does God need to be fair?
- ❖ Parable and allegory

Setting in the Gospel

This parable is one of Matthew's own parables. He does not derive it from Mark, as he does the parables of the sower, the mustard-seed, the wicked tenants and others. The final verse, 20:16, is reflected in 19:30, which reads: 'But many who are first will be last, and the last will be first.' This is not in fact the main point of the story. There is an awkwardness here, because this verse does not really fit with the parable.

The saying at beginning and end of the parable teaches a reversal of position: those who are successful in this world are not those who win success on Jesus' scale of values. The saying was originally meant to teach that those who give up everything for Christ will receive a bounteous reward (*Matthew* 19:29). Nor is the reversal of order of payment the point of the parable. The point of the story is actually the unpredictable generosity of the owner of the vineyard.

What kind of text?

This story is clearly a parable. While Mark's parables are mostly about nature and everyday objects, such as seeds, cloth, salt, water-bottles, this parable, like so many of the parables which Matthew chooses to insert, is about people. It is a contrast-story, in which different personalities are set in contrast against each other. Some of Matthew's parables are derived from Mark. Some are shared with Luke, and probably derived from a collection of sayings of Jesus. This is not one of them. Presumably Matthew drew it directly from the oral tradition of Jesus' teaching.

Parable of the Labourers in the Vineyard by Francesco Maffei (ca.1605-1660).

My beloved had a vineyard on a very fertile hill. He dug it and cleared it of stones, and planted it with choice vines; he built a watch-tower in the midst of it, and hewed out a wine vat in it; he expected it to yield grapes, but it yielded wild grapes. And now I will tell you what I will do to my vineyard. I will remove its hedge and it shall be devoured. I will break down its wall and it shall be trampled down. The vineyard of the Lord of hosts is the house of Israel, and the people of Judah are his pleasant planting.

Matthew attacks Pharisaic hypocrisy throughout chapter 23. The attack may well be partly as a warning to Christians to avoid the same distortion. Pharisees were as aware as anyone of the danger of hypocrisy. Rabbi Gamaliel II (the great teacher mentioned in Acts chapters 5 and 22) said: 'No student who thinks one thing and says another should be allowed in the school.' (Berakhot 28a) Rabbi Eliezer (about 270) said: 'A hypocrite brings anger upon the world.' (Sotah 41b)

Commentary: verse by verse reading

The Labourers are Hired

v.1 The vineyard is a favourite symbol of Israel. It was used already to criticise Israel by the prophet Hosea. Hosea 10:1 reads: 'Israel is a luxuriant vine that yields its fruit. The more his fruit increased, the more [idolatrous] altars he built.' Isaiah uses it first critically, in a haunting lament over Jerusalem. A much later poem in Isaiah, written either during or after the Babylonian exile (27:2-5), overturns the imagery of the vineyard laid waste, attesting the endurance of God's eager care to water the vineyard.

The same image is used in the parable of the wicked tenants. The Jewish authorities rightly see themselves portrayed as the ruffianly tenants of the vineyard who maltreat the messengers sent to them (*Matthew* 21:33-46).

In this parable of the labourers in the vineyard we may see a response by Jesus to the criticism of his opponents that he ate with tax-collectors and sinners. This criticism would come readily to the zealous and to those carefully obedient to the Law. In theory obedience to the Law was a pure act of love, a loving response in obedience to the Lord for the divine gift of the Law and of the choice to be his chosen people. In fact, it is only too easy for Christians, as well as for Pharisees, to slip over into the mentality of earning salvation.

Paul insists repeatedly, but especially when writing to the Galatians and Romans, on the impossibility of earning salvation. 'Justice', God's saving justice, is a gift of love by God, given to those who put their trust uniquely in God's saving power. It cannot be earned by good works.

For the Pharisees life was a tangle of commands and regulations, enwrapping all human activities. The more taxing it is to obey such rules, the more difficult it is to avoid a certain amount of complacency at having observed them. Only one more step takes you to the idea of earning salvation by good deeds.

v. 2 This verse has a special fascination because it is the only indication we have of the value of money in the time of Jesus: a denarius as the daily wage of a casual agricultural labourer. For the days before washing-machines, foreign holidays and expensive electronic gadgets it is difficult to give a modern equivalent. Oddly enough, although plenty of first-century coins have been unearthed in Israel, not one denarius from the time of Jesus has been found. Was Matthew's gospel written in Syria, and the name of a coin familiar there used?

vv.3-7 Following Roman usage, the day was divided into twelve 'hours' of sunlight. In the Mediterranean summer these would be roughly equivalent to 60 minutes of our time. The night did not have hours, but four 'watches' of the night, each roughly three modern hours long. The Greek text of the gospel says that the landowner goes out into the market-place at dawn, 'at the third hour' (mid-morning), 'at the sixth hour' (noon), 'at the ninth hour' (mid-afternoon) and 'at the eleventh hour', as the sun is beginning to set. One can already begin to feel the indignation of those who have toiled through the heat of the Palestine midday sun that anyone should even be employed for those paltry few minutes as the light begins to fail.

Deuteronomy 24:14-15

You shall not withhold the wages of poor and needy labourers. You shall pay them their wages daily before sunset, because they are poor and their livelihood depends on them. Otherwise they might cry to the Lord against you, and you would incur guilt.

The Payment is Made

vv.8-12 Bad enough that they should be employed! When pay-time came in the gathering dusk those who waited smugly at the end of the line must have been first of all stunned that the landowner should be so spendthrift as to shower coins on the late workers who had hardly got their hands dirty. Naturally they thought, 'In that case, what will there be for us?' As the paymaster works his way down the line, you can feel the rising indignation as each successive group gets paid – and still a single denarius.

vv.13-15 The very address is reproachful. The word translated 'Friend!' implies warmth of companionship. Matthew twice more uses it with an air of reproach and hurt: at the wedding-feast, 'Friend, how did you get in here without a wedding robe?' (22:12), and Jesus to Judas, 'Friend, do what you are here to do!' (26:50)

There is, then, an overtone of sadness: things should have gone better! Nor does it end in friendship, for the complainant is told 'Go!', or rather, more roughly, 'Take what is yours and off with you!' This is not an invitation into eternal companionship. Matthew thinks in sharp contrasts. We have seen earlier that almost all his own parables are contrast-parables, and his adjectives are crisp. Literally the Greek text does not read 'envious' and 'generous', but 'Is your eye wicked because I am good?' The story ends in sadness, not even in grudging acceptance.

v.16 So the reversal of the phrase which preceded the parable is ominous. In 19:30 'Many who are first will be last, and the last will be first' is a promise of hope to generous disciples. By contrast 'the last will be first, and the first will be last' is a threat.

St John Chrysostom comments:

In the kingdom of heaven there is no one who justifies himself or blames others in this way. That place is pure and free from envy and jealousy. For if the saints when they are here give their lives for sinners, how much more do they rejoice when they see them there enjoying rewards!

(Homily 64.3)

From St Gregory the Great:

Many are called but few are chosen. See how many have gathered for today's celebration: we fill the church. But yet who knows how few may be numbered in the flock of God's elect. All voices shout 'Christ', but not everyone's life shouts it. Many follow God with their voices but flee from him by their conduct.

(Forty Gospel Homilies, 19.5).

The Word Lives on

How should we evaluate this parable? Every instinct protests that the landowner's behaviour is not fair. On the other hand, he kept to his contract and the workers had no absolute right to complain.

Some parables are allegories. An allegory has several points of comparison, a parable only one. Is this an allegory or only a parable? Matthew certainly likes allegory. In the parable of the wicked tenants he emphasises the allegory by sending two sets of slaves, representing the earlier and later prophets (21:34-36), and by having the son ejected from the vineyard before – not after – he is killed, because Jesus was killed outside the city of Jerusalem (21:39). Some parables, however, cannot possibly be allegories. For instance, the final coming of the Lord likened to a thief in the night is a parable only, the single point of comparison being the unexpected swiftness. If the comparison were an allegory it would imply that the Lord had a dishonest purpose.

In this parable of the labourers in the vineyard the principal point is the unmotivated generosity of the landowner. Is the seeming unfairness also part of the intended teaching or not?

If the 'unfairness' is part of the intended meaning, the lesson is that you cannot enter into calculations with God, estimating what God owes you and what you owe God. Any reward is totally God's gift. It is not proportionate to any human merit.

The lesson that there is no such thing as fairness in bargaining with God is a hard one to swallow. It goes against all our notions of balance and merit. In the earlier books of the Old Testament long life and the prosperity of wealth were seen as the reward for fidelity. Eventually Israel could no longer blind itself to the truth that the wicked also live long and prosperously: such is the problem of the Book of Job, for Job rejects these ancient pious solutions.

Matthew 21:34-39 When the harvest time had come, he sent his slaves to the tenants to collect his produce. But the tenants seized his slaves and beat one, killed another, and stoned another. Again he sent other slaves, more than the first; and they treated them in the same way. Finally he sent his son to them, saying, 'They will respect my son.' But when the tenants saw the son, they said to themselves, 'This is the heir; come, let us kill him and get his inheritance.' So they seized the son, threw him out of the vineyard, and killed him.

Two parables in Matthew help us here. This parable contains the denial that you can bargain with God for working through the heat of the day. Another answer may be drawn from the parable of the unforgiving debtor (18:23-35). The debt which we owe to God is so great that there can be no question of deserts. We can only accept God's own forgiveness.

The parable of the labourers in the vineyard forms the gospel reading for the 25th Sunday in Ordinary Time in Year A. It is also read in the weekday lectionary on the Wednesday of the 20th Week of the Year.

The Workers in the Vineyard by Domenico Feti, (1589-1624).

Live the Word of God

What do you hear now?

Suggestions for reflection and prayer

Does God seem unjust? Am I right to rail against God? After all, Job and Jeremiah did. If God has treated you unfairly, you had better say so and sort it out. Am I truly innocent? Is there no crack in my armour? If nothing else, am I not becoming a richer, deeper, wiser person by the discipline and the suffering I undergo? Am I coming nearer to God? Do I not understand the Lord Jesus better?

If the first will be last and the last first, what position will I have? Have I been first or last? Have I exalted myself unduly? Have I used my talents in the service of the kingdom or uniquely for my own selfish advantage? Do those in my charge receive from me the care they would receive from Christ? What can I do to improve the situation?

- ❖ Pray for the wisdom to see how you can be a more Christlike figure.
- ❖ Pray for the endurance to be like Christ, despite the taunts and pinpricks of others.
- ❖ Pray for the love to see Christ in all those you meet, even the family!

If life is unfair to me, how much more unfair is it to refugees, to orphans, to the long-term handicapped, to prisoners of conscience, even to those who have got into a mess through their own stupidity or carelessness and want to pull themselves back up!

- ❖ Pray for all these.
- ❖ Pray for all those whom you know to be in misfortune.
- ❖ Pray for those who are trying to set things right in their lives.

St Paul speaks of God's actions in the following terms:

O the depth of the riches and wisdom and knowledge of God! How unsearchable are his judgements and how inscrutable his ways! For who has known the mind of the Lord? Or who has been his counsellor? Or who has given a gift to him, to receive a gift in return? For from him and through him and to him are all things. To him be the glory for ever. Amen.

(Romans 11:33-36)

The Last Judgment

Hear the Word of God

Read: Matthew 25:31-46

[31] 'When the Son of Man comes in his glory, and all the angels with him, then he will sit on the throne of his glory. [32] All the nations will be gathered before him, and he will separate people one from another as a shepherd separates the sheep from the goats, [33] and he will put the sheep at his right hand and the goats at the left. [34] Then the king will say to those at his right hand, 'Come, you that are blessed by my Father, inherit the kingdom prepared for you from the foundation of the world; [35] for I was hungry and you gave me food, I was thirsty and you gave me something to drink, I was a stranger and you welcomed me, [36] I was naked and you gave me clothing, I was sick and you took care of me, I was in prison and you visited me.' [37] Then the righteous will answer him, 'Lord, when was it that we saw you hungry and gave you food, or thirsty and gave you something to drink? [38] And when was it that we saw you a stranger and welcomed you, or naked and gave you clothing? [39] And when was it that we saw you sick or in prison and visited you?' [40] And the king will answer them, 'Truly I tell you, just as you did it to one of the least of these who are members of my family, you did it to me.' [41] Then he will say to those at his left hand, 'You that are accursed, depart from me into the eternal fire prepared for the devil and his angels; [42] for I was hungry and you gave me no food, I was thirsty and you gave me nothing to drink, [43] I was a stranger and you did not welcome me, naked and you did not give me clothing, sick and in prison and you did not visit me.' [44] Then they also will answer, 'Lord, when was it that we saw you hungry or thirsty or a stranger or naked or sick or in prison, and did not take care of you?' [45] Then he will answer them, 'Truly I tell you, just as you did not do it to one of the least of these, you did not do it to me.' [46] And these will go away into eternal punishment, but the righteous into eternal life.'

Opposite: The Seven Works of Mercy by Caravaggio.

Understand the Word of God

This session will explore:

- ❖ Apocalyptic writing in the New Testament
- ❖ The scenario of the Risen Christ as divine judge
- ❖ 'What you do to the least of these you do to me'
- ❖ Matthew's special emphasis on hell and punishment

Setting in the Gospel

This parable constitutes the final section of the gospel before we embark on the story of Jesus' death and resurrection. Mark was, of course, responsible for the outline of the three synoptic gospels, for Matthew and Luke followed carefully his pattern and order of events, adding their own proper sections, mostly drawn from a collection of sayings of the Lord. Mark ends Jesus' ministry with a full chapter (*Mark 13*) in which Jesus prepares his disciples for the future. He predicts the persecutions which the Church will undergo, and reassures them that they will be safe under the guidance of the Holy Spirit. Jesus promises that he will finally come in power to rescue his chosen ones from their trials. The Markan chapter is a highly structured discourse, each of the three sections being built on a scriptural quotation, in order to show that all this was foreseen and foretold in scripture. Mark does not tell us when the Son of Man will come to save his elect, but the whole chapter encourages the Church to be always on the alert, constantly repeating 'Beware!', 'Keep alert!', 'Keep awake!'.

Matthew expands this Markan chapter into the last of his five discourses in chapters 24-25. His most notable addition is the expansion of Mark's conclusion into four parables about staying awake and alert for the final judgment: the faithful servant, the watchful householder, the ten wedding-attendants and the talents. As the climax of the whole discourse he adds this fifth parable about the last judgment itself. Matthew takes it from the oral tradition, but includes significant editorial traits. For instance, there is the characteristic absolute contrast between the good, who are called 'the just', and the bad.

What kind of text?

Basically this is a parable rather than a description of a future event at the end of the world. It is certainly built on a parable of the sheep and the goats. It may have emerged in the ministry of Jesus as an answer to the question, 'What happens to those who have not heard the message of the gospel?' The parable is set within an apocalyptic framework, for Matthew frequently has his eye on the rewards and punishments at the end of time. Several of his parables treat of this theme: the net full of good and bad fish, the talents, the wheat and the darnel, and the labourers in the vineyard.

Apocalyptic is a way of writing which became popular in Judaism during the persecutions and repression of the two centuries before Jesus. It claims to reveal the secrets ('apocalypse' means 'revelation') of the future. It is a coded prediction, couched in biblical language and imagery, full of allusions to the Bible, number symbolism and bizarre images (rivers of blood, animals with horns and several heads, cosmic disturbances). The fullest biblical apocalypse is the Revelation of John (the last book of the Bible), but there are other snatches of apocalyptic in Isaiah, Ezekiel, especially the Book of Daniel, and also the gospels and a host of other non-biblical writings.

The purpose of apocalyptic is always to encourage the oppressed with a promise that God will not desert them in their sufferings, but will eventually deliver them in triumph and take them to himself in peace and joy.

Some examples of apocalyptic writing from the Book of Revelation:

5:6 Then I saw a lamb standing as if it had been slaughtered, having seven horns and seven eyes, which are the seven spirits of God sent out into all the earth.

6:12-13 I looked and there came a great earthquake; the sun became black as sackcloth, the full moon became like blood, and the stars of the sky fell to the earth as the fig-tree drops its winter fruit.

20:4-5 Then I saw thrones, and the souls of those who had been beheaded for their testimony to Jesus. They came to life and reigned with Christ.

Commentary: verse by verse reading

The Reward of the Blessed

v.31 Who is this Son of Man? We have seen that 'son of man' is a way in which Jesus reticently refers to himself, avoiding any hint of cult of personality or thrusting himself forward. Here, however, there is a crystal clear allusion to the 'one like a son of man' in the book of Daniel, who comes to receive all power from the Lord God. Also there is more, for the Son of Man is now himself seated on the throne (and the throne is always the throne of God) with his angels (and angels are always the angels of God) and his glory.

I saw one like a son of man coming with the clouds of heaven. And he came to the Ancient One and was presented before him. To him was given dominion and glory and kingship, that all peoples, nations and languages should serve him.

(Daniel 7:13-14).

In the Bible 'glory' is not just fame, recognition, acclaim, but is an awesome property of God. The divine glory is so overwhelming that the only possible human reaction is to hide and cower in reverent fear. 'We have seen his glory' in the Prologue of John (1:14) is an expression of the dread and daunting experience of the divinity of Jesus. Besides, throughout the Bible, in passage after passage, it is the Lord God who is judge. So here the Risen Lord Jesus Christ in his glory is enthroned as divine judge.

v.32 An important part of the Old Testament hope for the Messiah was the expectation that all nations would gather together at Jerusalem to derive salvation from her. This becomes more and more prominent in the messianic hope until the great judgement-scene in chapter 14 of the book of Zechariah. The opening of salvation to the whole universe was at the heart of Jesus' mission, bursting the bounds of Judaism and showing the face of God to all humanity. 'This idea of universality will turn up again and again as the real core of Jesus' mission', says Pope Benedict XVI (*Jesus of Nazareth*, p. 22).

Zechariah chapter 14 reads:

For I will gather all the nations against Jerusalem. Then the Lord will go forth and fight against those nations. On that day his feet shall stand on the Mount of Olives which lies before Jerusalem to the east.

(Zechariah 14:2-4)

In the Old Testament God is the shepherd of Israel, looking after his flock with loving care. In all the gospels, however, Jesus is seen as the shepherd. He is concerned for the masses who 'were like sheep without a shepherd' and feeds them in green pastures near restful waters (*Mark* 6:34-39). He is the good shepherd who knows his own and who lays down his life for his sheep (*John* 10:1-17).

The Lord is my shepherd, I shall not want.
He makes me lie down in green pastures,
he leads me beside still waters.
(Psalm 23:1-2)

v.33 The author knows his countryside lore. Sheep and goats are often included in the same flock in Palestine even today. But they tend to keep separate from each other, not liking each other's smell.

v.34 This is the only occasion in Matthew where Jesus is called 'the king' absolutely. Normally in the parables God is the king, for example, making a wedding banquet for his son (*Matthew* 22:1-10). For Jesus the kingdom which he came to renew and complete, the whole object of his mission, was the kingship of his Father. His vision was concentrated uniquely on this kingdom and on his Father, rather than on himself. Now he has taken his place as the Risen Christ in his glory. One is reminded of John 5:22: 'The Father judges no one but has given all judgment to the Son.' But the unity of the two persons in the godhead is shown by the fact that the blessed are still 'blessed by my Father'.

There is also a deal of comfort in the contrast between the two fates: for those who enter the inheritance, it has been prepared from the foundation of the world. The good is already planned and decreed. But, for those who are accursed, things have gone terribly wrong. The eternal fire was prepared not for them but for the devil and his angels.

Goats and sheep grazing, see v.33 above.

Matthew 10:42 Whoever gives even a cup of cold water to one of these little ones in the name of a disciple – truly I tell you, none of these will lose their reward.

Acts 9:4-5 Saul, Saul, why do you persecute me? 'Who are you, Lord?' I am Jesus whom you are persecuting.

vv.35-40 Lists of good works occur in other literatures. The Egyptian 'Book of the Dead' represents the dead protesting their innocence and claiming 'I have given bread to the hungry, water to the thirsty, clothed the naked'. The startling originality of our passage is that the sheep remain silent and the initiative comes from the judge. The judge himself speaks, complementing them on their good works – to their own surprise, or, in the opposite case, their indignation!

The reward is the fulfilment of the promises in such passages as Matthew 10:42. Matthew has, of course, taught insistently that Christ is present in his Church, and deep in Paul's thought is the insistence that Christ is present in the individual Christian. What is done to the Christian is done to Christ himself.

In this scene the judgment is based uniquely on how we treat those in need. This criterion includes, of course, all social relationships, all of which consist in responding to the needs and rights of other people. In other passages a criterion is firmness of witness to Christ or perseverance under trial. In the gospel of John the only criterion for moral behaviour is love, but at the same time again and again in the gospel people are judged by their acceptance or rejection of Jesus.

The Last Judgement by Fra Angelico.

The Fate of the Accursed

vv.41-46 It is striking that of all the major writers of the New Testament, Matthew is the most forceful about eternal punishment. Paul and John do not mention it, perhaps because their horizon is so filled by the triumph of Christ that there is no room for other aspects. Paul teaches amply (notably in 1 *Corinthians* 15) about the resurrection and transformation of those who are in Christ, after the model of the Risen Christ himself. In John Jesus teaches repeatedly about eternal life, and proclaims that he is the resurrection and life (*John* 11:25). In neither of these authors is there a word about what happens to those who do not rise in Christ.

If we had only these two authors in the New Testament, we might think that only the blessed rise again or continue in life, and that others cease to exist at death. In Matthew, on the other hand, just as human beings are sharply divided into the good and the bad, the righteous and the unrighteous, producing good or bad fruit, so the outcome of their lives is either heaven or hell.

In Mark 9:43-47 there is mention of Gehenna (the visual image of hell, the evil-smelling rubbish-dump outside Jerusalem, where fires were perpetually burning). But Matthew adds further dimensions. The threat of separation by the angels, of fire, the day of judgment, weeping and gnashing of teeth are almost wholly confined to Matthew in the New Testament.

In other words, apart from the even-handed Matthew, it is the positive rather than the negative outcome, the rewards rather than the punishments, that receive the heavier emphasis in the New Testament.

Only the two letters of Peter, also strongly influenced by Jewish apocalyptic, have anything like so vivid a conception of punishment in the after-life.

In chapter 2 of the Second Letter of Peter we read:

If God did not spare the angels when they sinned, but cast them into hell and committed them to chains of deepest darkness to be kept until the judgment .... then the Lord knows how to rescue the godly from trial, and to keep the unrighteous under punishment until the day of judgment.

(verses 4 and 9)

The Word Lives on

The two key phrases in the parable are 'Come, you that are blessed by my Father' and 'Depart from me'. It is important not to halt at the apocalyptic imagery employed by Matthew. The importance of the glorious vision of the exalted Christ with which the scene begins is that the true joy of heaven is companionship with Christ and with the Lord God. The misery of the other extreme is separation from God, from all that is lovable.

Artists, poets and musicians have at different times attempted to convey these two extremes by various symbolisms, of which fiery torment is only one image. It is perhaps more satisfactory to recall Paul's quotation of the words of the prophet Isaiah: 'What no eye has seen, nor ear heard, nor the human heart conceived, what God has prepared for those who love him' (1 *Corinthians* 2:9).

The secret of heaven is to be enveloped in the love of God, and the whole of scripture struggles to give even an inadequate impression of that love under such terms as a father's love (as in *Hosea* 11:1-4 and *Luke* 15:11-32, the parable of the prodigal son), a mother's love (as expressed in *Isaiah* 66:10-11), and the love of a courting couple (*Song of Songs*). Sitting on a cloud is less important than who one is sitting next to! Playing a harp is less important than communicating with an appreciative divine audience!

This great judgment scene forms the gospel reading for the Feast of Christ the King in Year A. It is read also on Monday of the First Week of Lent to suggest a framework for the endeavours of Lent.

Live the Word of God

Listen again to the reading: Matthew 25:31-46

What do you hear now?

Suggestions for reflection and prayer

Do I spend enough time and effort in prayer to the glorified Christ, our Saviour and the King of the universe?

❖ Pray that the centrality of the exalted Christ may be recognised by all people.

❖ Pray that when he comes as judge he may find us ready.

❖ Pray for insight into your own strengths and weaknesses.

Do I see Christ in the poor and unfortunate? Do I actively take part in the Church's 'option for the poor'? Could I do more, either for those near me or for those in more distant lands?

❖ Pray for the sick, the housebound, especially those without help.

❖ Pray for refugees and the starving, especially in the drought-stricken areas of the world.

❖ Pray for prisoners, both unjustly and justly imprisoned.

From St John Chrysostom:

For even though you should meet your enemy, is not his suffering enough to overcome and subdue your resistance to being merciful? What about his hunger, cold, chains, nakedness and sickness? You could at once have befriended him and done good. Even when you see a dog hungry you feel sympathy. But when you see the Lord hungry, you ignore it.

(Homily 79)

Jesus in Gethsemane

Hear the Word of God

Read: Matthew 26:36-56

36 Then Jesus went with them to a place called Gethsemane; and he said to his disciples, 'Sit here while I go over there and pray.' 37 He took with him Peter and the two sons of Zebedee, and began to be grieved and agitated. 38 Then he said to them, 'I am deeply grieved, even to death; remain here, and stay awake with me.' 39 And going a little farther, he threw himself on the ground and prayed, 'My Father, if it is possible, let this cup pass from me; yet not what I want but what you want.' 40 Then he came to the disciples and found them sleeping; and he said to Peter, 'So, could you not stay awake with me one hour? 41 Stay awake and pray that you may not come into the time of trial; the spirit indeed is willing, but the flesh is weak.' 42 Again he went away for the second time and prayed, 'My Father, if this cannot pass unless I drink it, your will be done.' 43 Again he came and found them sleeping, for their eyes were heavy. 44 So leaving them again, he went away and prayed for the third time, saying the same words. 45 Then he came to the disciples and said to them, 'Are you still sleeping and taking your rest? See, the hour is at hand, and the Son of Man is betrayed into the hands of sinners. 46 Get up, let us be going. See, my betrayer is at hand.'

47 While he was still speaking, Judas, one of the twelve, arrived; with him was a large crowd with swords and clubs, from the chief priests and the elders of the people. 48 Now the betrayer had given them a sign, saying, 'The one I will kiss is the man; arrest him.' 49 At once he came up to Jesus and said, 'Greetings, Rabbi!' and kissed him. 50 Jesus said to him, 'Friend, do what you are here to do.' Then they came and laid hands on Jesus and arrested him. 51 Suddenly, one of those with Jesus put his hand on his sword, drew it, and struck the slave of the high priest, cutting off his ear. 52 Then Jesus said to him, 'Put your sword back into its place; for all who take the sword will perish by the sword. 53 Do you think that I cannot appeal to my Father, and he will at once send me more than twelve legions of angels? 54 But how then would the scriptures be fulfilled, which say it must happen in this way?' 55 At that hour Jesus said to the crowds, 'Have you come out with swords and clubs to arrest me as though I were a bandit? Day after day I sat in the temple teaching, and you did not arrest me. 56 But all this has taken place, so that the scriptures of the prophets may be fulfilled.' Then all the disciples deserted him and fled.

Opposite: Jesus Praying in Gethsemane Vladimir Mazuranic (b.1910).

Understand the Word of God

This session will explore:

- ❖ the formation of the narrative
- ❖ Jesus' very human dread of the passion, and his obedience
- ❖ the motivation of Judas
- ❖ the fulfilment of scripture in the Passion Narrative

Setting in the Gospel

In the narrative of the agony of Jesus in the garden we see Jesus preparing, in full consciousness, for the ordeal which lies before him. He braces himself to fulfil the task before him of obedience to the Father's will. This is our first section of the Passion Narrative, which is found in chapters 26 and 27 of the gospel.

In Mark's account, on which Matthew builds, we see a very human Jesus almost beside himself with horror and dread at the approaching passion. Matthew tones down Mark's strong words. Nevertheless, this is the essential moment which sets the scene for the passion. Jesus is at his most vulnerable, but commits himself fully to his Father's will.

A triple repetition emphasises the main point. Three times Jesus finds the disciples sleeping and there will be three denials by Peter. The theme of the failure of the disciples is strong.

There was a steady tradition of Jesus' agonised prayer before the passion, which appears also in the Letter to the Hebrews. Mark may well have built up the scene to express his own inspired understanding of the event, and Matthew followed him.

In the Letter to the Hebrews we read:

In the days of his flesh Jesus offered up prayers and supplications, with loud cries and tears, to the one who was able to save him from death, and he was heard because of his reverent submission.

(Hebrews 5:7)

What kind of text?

It has been held that the Passion Narrative is the oldest part of the gospel. The earliest presentation of the passion is a short outline given in 1 Corinthians 15:3-5. This was a piece of tradition which Paul himself learnt by heart and passed on to his converts.

The Jewish historian Josephus also tells us that Jesus was crucified by the Romans on the orders of Pontius Pilate at the instigation of the Jewish authorities. Both these historical outlines refer to the fulfilment of the scriptures concerning Jesus.

It has been held that it would have been impossible to proclaim the good news of Christ without a fairly substantial account of his passion, death and resurrection, and that therefore this must have been developed at the very beginning of the Christian movement. More recent studies, however, indicate that much of the Passion Narrative must have been pulled together and composed from a sketchy oral tradition by Mark himself. After all, the disciples deserted Jesus at an early stage.

Matthew largely follows Mark, with some elaborations of his own, as we will see.

1 Corinthians 15:3-5:

For I handed on to you as of first importance what I in turn had received: that Christ died for our sins in accordance with the scriptures, and that he was buried, and that he was raised on the third day in accordance with the scriptures, and that he appeared to Cephas, then to the twelve.

Many believe that the words of Josephus about Christ have been edited by Christians. Josephus here sounds like a Christian himself, and his original text may well have been less positive about Jesus.

When Pilate, on the indictment of the principal men among us, had Jesus condemned to the cross, those who loved him at the first did not cease to do so, for he appeared to them again alive on the third day, the divine prophets having foretold these and ten thousand other wonderful things about him.

(Antiquities xviii.64)

Gethsemane by Jesus Mafa.

Commentary: verse by verse reading

The Agony in the Garden

v.36 Those who celebrated the passover supper were obliged to spend the night in Jerusalem. According to Josephus, who often exaggerates, a million-and-a-half pilgrims went up to Jerusalem for the feast. In any case, by a legal fiction the bounds of Jerusalem were enlarged to include the Mount of Olives, the hill over against Jerusalem to the east. As its name implies, it was a mass of olive trees, and no one knows the exact location of Gethsemane, which means 'garden of oil'. The traditional spot was chosen for the convenience of pilgrims on the road to Jericho!

The Garden of Gethsemane, John Millar Watt, (1895-1975) / Private Collection / © Look and Learn.

v.37 Jesus takes with him the three who form the inner core of the disciples. These three had been chosen to witness the raising of Jairus' daughter, as narrated in Mark's account, and the Transfiguration. The two sons of Zebedee had also been squabbling about seats on either side of Jesus, though Matthew puts the request on their mother's lips (*Matthew* 20:20). They see Jesus at his high point and his low point.

Mark uses two very strong words about Jesus' frame of mind. Mark's word in 14:33 translated 'distressed' can almost mean 'stunned'. Matthew tones this down, referring to Jesus as 'grieved and agitated', out of respect for Jesus' dignity, but in so doing he reduces the horror which Jesus withstood. Luke reduces it still further, showing Jesus deliberately kneeling for his prayer and standing up at the end of it – the model of earnest Christian prayer (*Luke* 22:41-45).

v.38 Matthew adds the phrase 'with me' to 'stay awake' both here and in verse 40, thereby underlining how the disciples should share their master's suffering, and suggesting also that the master will be present with them in their trials.

v.39 Jesus' attitude, literally 'he fell face to the ground', is no mere gesture, but is the position of desperate prayer. It is also the attitude of utter reverence. Matthew's only other use of the expression is of the disciples in 17:6 on hearing the voice at the Transfiguration.

At the same time there is a wonderful intimacy in the address, 'My father'. Mark here uses the Aramaic word *Abba*. This is not, as has often been said, a child's call of 'Daddy!' It is a dignified adult word of close family affection. In Matthew Jesus repeatedly refers to God as 'my father', but only here and in verse 42 does he address him directly as 'My father!', the sign of intimacy and obedience. In the early Christian community it was felt to be of such significance that it was retained in Aramaic as a sort of talisman, attesting that Christians may use the title in virtue of their adoption.

vv.40-41 In Mark 14:37 the leader of the Twelve bears the full brunt of Jesus' reproach when Jesus says, 'Simon, are you asleep?' In Matthew he is spared a little, for Jesus, addressing Peter, says 'Could you (plural) not stay awake with me one hour?' They are therefore all implicated in the same blame. They are, however, spared the reproach given in Mark, 'they did not know what to say to him' (14:40). Matthew does not like to paint too black a picture of the leaders of the Christian Church, and several times weakens the reproaches that Jesus makes to them.

Paul too makes reference to the use of Abba in prayer.

You did not receive a spirit of slavery to fall back into fear, but you received a spirit of adoption. When we cry, 'Abba! Father!' it is that very Spirit bearing witness with our spirit that we are children of God.

(Romans 8:15-16)

St Jerome writes:

It is impossible for the human soul to avoid temptation. Hence we say in the Lord's Prayer, 'Lead us not into temptation' which we are unable to withstand. We do not refuse to face temptation entirely but pray for the strength to bear up under it. Therefore he does not say, 'Watch and pray that you may not be tempted' but 'that you may not enter into temptation,' that is, that temptation may not overwhelm you and hold you in its grip.

(Commentary on Matthew 4.26.41)

Other texts concerning the hour in John's gospel:

John 2:4 My hour has not yet come.

John 17:1 Father, the hour has come; glorify your Son so that your Son may glorify you.

vv.42-43 Jesus' second prayer repeats his first, but adds 'Thy will be done', as in the prayer he taught his disciples. It is especially touching that he himself, at his moment of direst need, should join all Christians in this prayer, giving this petition a special depth of meaning. By contrast, this time Jesus seems to have remained in his loneliness, for he does not disturb the sleeping disciples.

vv.44-46 For the third prayer we are given no further details, but when Jesus returns to the disciples he moves swiftly from leaving them asleep to rousing them with words which are reminiscent of John: 'The hour has come' (*John* 12:23) and 'Rise, let us be on our way' (*John* 14:31). Matthew seems to be introducing the Johannine theology of the 'hour', that moment to which Jesus looks forward throughout his ministry, the hour of his exaltation and glorification, which is to occur by his suffering and death. Jesus' knowledge, before Judas appears, that his betrayer is at hand is a final indication of his acceptance of the Father's will.

Kiss of Judas from St. Mark's Basilica.

The Arrest

v.47 Judas is presumably needed to lead the arresting party to the right group. On this night there would have been many other groups bivouacking or otherwise passing the night of Passover on the Mount of Olives. It is noteworthy that Matthew, himself a scribe (13:52), omits Mark's inclusion of 'scribes' in the arresting party. This is no business of the 'scribes', who were lawyers. Jesus' controversies about interpretation of the law are now over.

Nor do the Pharisees play any part in the passion and death of Jesus, despite their disagreements with him about the interpretation of the Law. 'The chief priests and the elders of the people' are those who come to arrest Jesus. There is a concern among the temple authorities to avoid another scene in the temple during the festival time.

vv.48-50 The focus is upon Judas' treachery. As at the Last Supper the focus had been upon the betrayal of sharing the same dish rather than on the identification of the traitor, so now it is on betrayal of friendship. Judas greets and kisses Jesus. Significantly, however, he does not call Jesus 'Lord', as in Matthew all disciples do. His choice of the title 'Rabbi' certifies that he is no longer a disciple.

Matthew will describe the suicide of Judas in 27:3-10 in terms of that of Ahitophel, the only suicide in the Hebrew Bible, who was companion and adviser to David, and who also betrayed his master (2 *Samuel* 17:23).

Jesus replies with the sad address 'Friend!' In Matthew this always seems to imply a gentle reproach (as in 20:13 and 22:12). The rest of his reply is puzzling, literally 'For what you are present'. Is it a question or (as NRSV) a command?

Matthew 20:13 But he replied to one of them, 'Friend, I am doing you no wrong; did you not agree with me for the usual daily wage?'

Matthew 22:12 He said to him, 'Friend, how did you get in here without a wedding robe?'

What was Judas' motive? His name 'Judas' might suggest that he was a militant nationalist, for Judas the Maccabee was the leader of Jewish resistance against the Syrian oppression two hundred years before. Perhaps, when he realised that Jesus was not a political Messiah, he lost interest and decided to sell him to the authorities. Nothing confirms this. The Gospel of John says that as the treasurer he was avaricious and dishonest (*John* 12:6).

The recently-published 'Gospel of Judas' is a second-century document, a valuable witness to second-century thought, but without historical worth for Jesus and Judas.

It grapples with the problem of why Judas betrayed Jesus. It emerged from the circles of the Gnostics, who developed their particular off-shoot of Christianity in the early centuries. Their works were very soon regarded as heretical.

It has been pointed out that Mark, the earliest gospel, does not call Judas a 'traitor', but only says that he 'handed Jesus over'. This has been interpreted as 'arranging a meeting' with the high priest, so that he and Jesus could sort out their differences. This went disastrously wrong. So Judas would have committed suicide because of his well-meaning failure, but was subsequently demonised as a traitor.

vv.51-53 The incident with the sword provides an occasion for Jesus' teaching. In Mark the sword is wielded by 'one of the bystanders', not one of Jesus' own group. Jesus seems to intervene to heal a mere chance wound in the fracas of arrest. In Matthew the sword is wielded by 'one of those with Jesus', identified in John as Peter (*John* 18:10).

This gives Jesus the opportunity to reject violence as a solution. In the Sermon on the Mount he had rejected retaliation ('an eye for an eye' 5:38). Now, making use of the opportunity of his own case to continue his teaching, he rejects it even more strongly. The twelve legions of angels, another example of typical Matthean exaggeration, like the ten thousand talents of 18:24, would amount to the staggering figure of 72,000 angels, a divine army capable of outfacing any opposition! Jesus' method is of open and peaceful teaching in the temple.

vv.54-56 Finally Matthew underlines that all this was to fulfil the scriptures. Writing for Christians sprung from Judaism he loses no opportunity to stress such fulfilment, using this formula fourteen times in his gospel, 'so that the scriptures of the prophets may be fulfilled'. It almost seems in Matthew that to Jesus fulfilling the scriptures was more important than healing the sick or spreading the good news.

Numerous details of the Passion Narrative are recounted in such a way that this fulfilment is made clear. Jesus has already quoted Zachariah 13:7, 'I will strike the shepherd and the sheep of the flock will be scattered', which is about to be fulfilled. Many more allusions will follow, such as Jesus' silence before his accusers, both Jewish and Roman, fulfilling the sheep, silent before its shearers, in Isaiah 53:7.

The desertion by the disciples must have been one of the worst aspects of Jesus' Passion. His purpose was to establish the kingdom or kingship of God, to renew this sovereignty in a new Israel. The crowds did not respond, so he chose the Twelve as a nucleus of the new Israel, twelve new foundation-stones. Of the Twelve one betrays him, one denies him three times, and the rest desert him. In the end, therefore, Jesus is alone, with all his attempts to establish his Father's will seemingly in tattered ruins. Yet it is by accepting this obedience that Jesus saves the world.

On the road to Emmaus the Risen Christ himself explains how the Passion is the fulfilment of 'all the scriptures' (Luke 24:27), and in the oldest tradition – a piece learnt by heart by Paul, and passed on by him – the events are 'in accordance with the scriptures' (1 Corinthians 15:3). We can see that this fulfilment is in accord not merely with individual snippets of scripture, but with the whole thrust of God's plan as revealed in the scripture.

Jesus' violent death was not the result of chance in an unfortunate coincidence of circumstances, but is part of the mystery of God's plan, as Peter explains in his first sermon on Pentecost: 'This Jesus was delivered up according to the definite plan and foreknowledge of God.' This biblical language does not mean that those who handed him over were merely passive players in a scenario written in advance by God.

(Catechism of the Catholic Church, n. 599)

Judas Betrays his Master, from a bible printed by Edward Gover, 1870's , Siegfried Detler Bendixen, (1786-1864).

The Word Lives on

The Passion Narrative in Matthew's gospel is read on Passion (Palm) Sunday in Year A. It does not occur in any other reading at Mass.

It has been set to music most notably by Johann Sebastian Bach in his 'St Matthew Passion'. Bach also set to music the Passion Narrative in John's gospel, which is read liturgically on Good Friday.

The Arrest of Christ, from the Hours of Etienne Chevalier, c.1445, Jean Fouquet, (c.1420-80).

Live the Word of God

Listen again to the reading: Matthew 26:36-56

What do you hear now?
Suggestions for reflection and prayer

If my prayer to be delivered from suffering and/or persecution is not answered, why not? What must I do to make this suffering fruitful and oriented to God? Do I meaningfully join my paltry sufferings with those of Christ? What can I do to help those who find suffering, bereavement, frustration unbearable?

❖ Pray for those who suffer.

❖ Pray for those who cannot understand their suffering as God's call.

❖ Pray for a deeper understanding of your own inadequacies.

When I am tempted do I turn to the Lord? What can I do to bring under control my regular temptations? Do I pray about them and ask the Lord's help in due time, or only panic when they occur? Would it help to communicate them to a confessor or other trusted person?

❖ Pray for all who are tempted beyond their strength.

❖ Pray for God's strength, guidance and wisdom to conquer your own temptations.

❖ Pray for the wisdom and tolerance to help others who are tempted.

Do I impose my will by violence, physical or psychological? Do I exert undue pressure on those under my control? Do I do what I can to diminish violence in the world, in politics and in families? Do people find in me a person of peace and generosity?

❖ Pray for peace in the world, peace between nations and peace within nations.

❖ Pray for peace in family life, especially between spouses and between parents and children.

❖ Pray for those who suffer violence and for those who live by violence.

The following Chorale is taken from Bach's 'St Matthew Passion':

O Father, let Thy will be done,
For all things well Thou doest,
In time of need refusest none,
But helpest e'en the lowest.
In deep distress,
Thou still dost bless,
In wrath, rememberest mercy;
Who trusts in Thee shall ever be
In perfect peace and safety.

The Crucifixion, Death
and Burial of Jesus

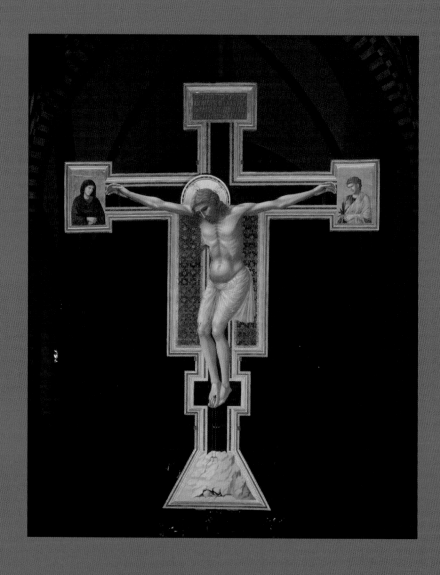

Hear the Word of God

Read: Matthew 27:45-66

[45] From noon on, darkness came over the whole land until three in the afternoon. [46] And about three o'clock Jesus cried with a loud voice, 'Eli, Eli, lema sabachthani?' that is, 'My God, my God, why have you forsaken me?' [47] When some of the bystanders heard it, they said, 'This man is calling for Elijah.' [48] At once one of them ran and got a sponge, filled it with sour wine, put it on a stick, and gave it to him to drink. [49] But the others said, 'Wait, let us see whether Elijah will come to save him.' [50] Then Jesus cried again with a loud voice and breathed his last. [51] At that moment the curtain of the temple was torn in two, from top to bottom. The earth shook, and the rocks were split. [52] The tombs also were opened, and many bodies of the saints who had fallen asleep were raised. [53] After his resurrection they came out of the tombs and entered the holy city and appeared to many. [54] Now when the centurion and those with him, who were keeping watch over Jesus, saw the earthquake and what took place, they were terrified and said, 'Truly this man was God's Son!'

[55] Many women were also there, looking on from a distance; they had followed Jesus from Galilee and had provided for him. [56] Among them were Mary Magdalene, and Mary the mother of James and Joseph, and the mother of the sons of Zebedee.

[57] When it was evening, there came a rich man from Arimathea, named Joseph, who was also a disciple of Jesus. [58] He went to Pilate and asked for the body of Jesus; then Pilate ordered it to be given to him. [59] So Joseph took the body and wrapped it in a clean linen cloth [60] and laid it in his own new tomb, which he had hewn in the rock. He then rolled a great stone to the door of the tomb and went away. [61] Mary Magdalene and the other Mary were there, sitting opposite the tomb.

[62] The next day, that is, after the day of Preparation, the chief priests and the Pharisees gathered before Pilate [63] and said, 'Sir, we remember what that impostor said while he was still alive, 'After three days I will rise again.' [64] Therefore command that the tomb be made secure until the third day; otherwise his disciples may go and steal him away, and tell the people, 'He has been raised from the dead', and the last deception would be worse than the first.' [65] Pilate said to them, 'You have a guard of soldiers; go, make it as secure as you can.' [66] So they went with the guard and made the tomb secure by sealing the stone.

Opposite: Crucifix by Giotto (1266-1336).

Understand the Word of God

This session will explore:

- ❖ the nature and tone of the account
- ❖ Jesus' last words in Matthew
- ❖ the hostility to Judaism
- ❖ burial and tombs

Setting in the Gospel

The desire to embrace his Father's plan of redeeming love inspired Jesus' whole life, for his redemptive passion was the very reason for his Incarnation. Jesus is at the same time the suffering Servant who silently allows himself to be led to the slaughter, and who bears the sin of the multitudes, and also the Paschal Lamb, the symbol of Israel's redemption at the first Passover.

(Catechism of the Catholic Church, n. 607-8)

A famous description of the gospels was 'Passion Narratives with extended introductions'. All through the gospel the crucifixion has been looming on the horizon, like a dark cloud, with the light of the resurrection about to break through. The myrrh given to the child Jesus by the magi in Matthew 2:11 has traditionally been interpreted as a presage of his death and burial. After the earliest controversies 'the Pharisees went out and conspired against him, how to destroy him' (*Matthew* 12:14). As soon as Peter has acknowledged Jesus as Messiah comes the first of the three great, formal prophecies of the Passion (*Matthew* 16:21). Again after the Transfiguration comes the qualification that they are not to tell anyone 'until after the Son of Man has been raised from the dead' (*Matthew* 17:9). Now the inevitable happens.

What kind of text?

This story is indeed history, a fuller version of what was told both by Paul's traditional summary in 1 Corinthians 15:1-8, and by the Jewish historian Josephus. But a historical account is always interpretative, and in this case some elements are certainly interpretative, giving the sense of events. We simply do not know how much is founded on historical memory, and how much is derived from the understanding of the event in the Christian community, as Christians reflected that 'it must have happened like this'. The whole difficulty of interpreting the gospels is that you get two statements of completely different type right next to each other. Jesus died (historical fact in 27:50), and the veil of the Temple was split (apocalyptic interpretation in 27:51).

Commentary: verse by verse reading

The Death of Jesus

v.45 The darkness at Jesus' death has provoked a vain search in astronomical records for an eclipse on the date of the crucifixion. It has also led to an appeal to a desert dust-storm. Such dust-storms do occur in the desert around Eastertime, with frightening ten metre visibility, but Jerusalem is not in the desert! Darkness at noon is a reference to Amos' prophecy of the Day of the Lord, that terrifying day when the Lord will visit the earth at the end of time to right all wrongs and fully establish his kingship (*Amos* 8:9). Amos describes it in terms of cosmic upheaval and great distress.

The Christian believes that the crucifixion and the resurrection constituted this earth-shattering event when God visited his people and changed everything for ever, the definitive moment of the conquest of evil. This was the moment that changed the world. There may perhaps also be an allusion to the darkness at noon in Egypt at the ninth plague, which lasted three days, which is narrated in Exodus 10:22. This would point to the crucifixion as the moment of the freeing of God's people from slavery.

Amos 8:9 On that day, says the Lord God, I will make the sun go down at noon, and darken the earth in broad daylight. I will turn your feasts into mourning and all your songs into lamentation.

Exodus 10:22 So Moses stretched out his hand towards heaven, and there was dense darkness in all the land of Egypt for three days.

v.46 Mark divides this day of days into three-hour segments, and speaks of the third hour (*Mark* 15:25), the sixth hour (15:33), and the ninth hour (15:33). Matthew, in following Mark, omits the third hour. It has been suggested that these times may be connected to the hours of prayer in the temple, but there is insufficient evidence of these times of prayer. The influence is probably in the other direction: Christian prayer-times were founded on this division.

Jesus' great cry is given by Mark in Aramaic (*Eloi, eloi…*) and by Matthew in Hebrew (*Eli, eli…*). In fact, the bystanders' confusion with Elijah then becomes more intelligible. In isolation this is a cry of dereliction, on which some gruesome theologies have been founded: that Jesus felt himself to be utterly deserted by his Father, that he suffered the pains of the damned, and eventually (in the twelfth century) that the Father exacted from his Son the penalty due for sin.

Any faithful Jew who lived by the Bible as Jesus did would know that it is the intonation of Psalm 22. This psalm, more than any other, is the clue to the Passion Narrative: it moves through the agonised suffering of God's faithful servant to the triumph of God and the vindication of the servant. Exactly this movement must have been going through Jesus' mind.

We have already considered the importance of scriptural allusions in the formation of the Passion Narrative, and Psalm 22 is cited twice more at the division of Jesus' clothes in verse 35, and the mockery by the passers-by in verse 39. This fills in the details of the scene, but also underlines that the event fulfils the scriptures.

In Luke's gospel Jesus' last cry, 'Father, into your hands I commend my spirit' (23:46), has scriptural reference in the confident trust in the Lord of Psalm 31:5. John relies on other traditions and builds a scene with different emphases (*John* 19).

v.47 The bystanders mistake Jesus' cry of 'Eli' as a shortened form of 'Eliyahu' (the Hebrew name of the prophet Elijah). This could be a reference to the popular idea that Elijah would come to rescue the pious in difficulties. More likely, in Matthew's thinking, would be a

Relevant verses from Psalm 22:

My God, my God, why have you forsaken me? Why are you so far from helping me? … They divide my clothing among themselves, and for my clothing they cast lots. … They shake their heads: 'Commit your cause to the Lord, let him rescue the one in whom he delights!'

(verses 1, 10, 7-8)

reference to the idea of Elijah as the prophet who would return to usher in the last times, as suggested in the Book of Malachi.

v.48 It is difficult to know whether the offer of 'sour wine' to Jesus was intended as a taunt or as a gesture of compassion. It could refer to the cheap wine beloved of soldiers, which was safer to drink than water in those days. The word used really means 'vinegar', which brings in the reference to Psalm 69:21, a hostile gesture of taunt against the just man by the impious. This is intensified by Matthew with the bystander's sarcastic words: 'Stop! Let's see whether Elijah comes to save him.'

Particularly in the Passion Narrative Matthew highlights Jewish hostility. He shows the authorities stirring up the crowd to secure not only Barabbas' release, but Jesus' crucifixion (27:20), Pilate washing his hands of all responsibility (27:24), and the mocking chief priests actually using the scriptural taunts of the wicked against the just man (27:43). Matthew was writing for a community of Christians sprung from Judaism, who were being harried by their non-Christian fellow-Jews, and he frequently allows this hostility to be reflected in his writing.

v.50 In a hard world where life was cheap the death of Jesus is told in a matter-of-fact way. The account has made no attempt to stir the emotions or depict the horror of this dreadful mode of execution, all too familiar in the Roman 'civilization' of the time. The accent is all on interpreting what happened.

Lo, I will send you the prophet Elijah before the great and terrible day of the Lord comes.

(Malachi 4:5)

A document of the Pontifical Biblical Commission reads:

The good news, accepted wholeheartedly in the beginning by many Jews, met with opposition from the leaders, who were eventually followed by the greater part of the people. The result was that between Jewish and Christian communities a situation of conflict arose that clearly left its mark on the redaction of the gospels and Acts.

(The Jewish People and their Sacred Scriptures in the Christian Bible, n.70)

The Crucifixion by Lorenzo Monaco, (c.1370-1425).

The free gift is not like the trespass. For if the many died through the one man's trespass, much more surely have the grace of God and the free gift in the grace of the one man, Jesus Christ, abounded for the many. For just as by the one man's disobedience the many were made sinners, so by the one man's obedience the many will be made righteous. (Romans 5 verses 15 and 19)

When Jesus had received the wine he said, 'It is finished.' Then he bowed his head and gave up his spirit. (John 18:30)

Paul, in discussing the work of Christ in Romans 5:12-21, stresses that death spread to all through sin, Adam's sin, the sin of humanity, but concentrates not so much on Christ's own death as on his obedience. It is the obedience of Jesus, the one perfect representative of humanity, that overcomes the disobedience of Adam, the representative and icon of fallen humanity. The secret of the cross is not in the bloodshed itself, but in the obedience even as far as bloodshed.

The words for 'Jesus breathed his last' could also be understood 'Jesus let go his spirit'. Is there already a hint, which will become clearer in John, that Jesus 'gave over his Spirit', the gift of the Spirit of Jesus which will vivify the new Christian community?

vv.51-53 The tearing of the veil of the temple signifies the end of the mystique of Judaism, or perhaps that Judaism's special access to God in the Holy of Holies is now thrown open to all. Matthew himself inserts the cosmic disturbances and the opening of the tombs. It does not of course mean that the skeletons walked into Jerusalem, but that the crucifixion opened the way for the sacred dead to enter the heavenly Jerusalem.

Fresco of the Resurrection in the Chora Church, Istanbul.

This is Matthew's way – in the mode of Jewish apocalyptic – of describing what later became poetically known as 'the Harrowing of Hell'. This is a visual way of describing and conveying the effects of Jesus' death. It is wonderfully depicted, especially in the art of the Eastern Churches, by Jesus grasping Adam by the hand and drawing him out of his tomb. There is a slight time-difficulty in the gospel account: what did these raised sacred dead do between the death of Jesus and his resurrection?

v.54 Just as at the baptism of Jesus Matthew turns Mark's private experience of Jesus into a public scene, so here he turns the centurion's statement into a public reaction. At the baptism Mark has Jesus alone experience the voice from heaven, 'You are my beloved Son', (*Mark* 1:11), which Matthew makes audible to those present, 'This is my beloved Son' (*Matthew* 3:17). Now at the death of Jesus, while Mark has the centurion alone make his declaration about Jesus (*Mark* 15:39), Matthew shows 'the centurion and those with him' reflecting on the occurrences, moved by the death of Jesus and the accompanying events.

The cosmos itself is participating in the events. The auxiliary troops controlling the execution will have been from another part of the Roman Empire, not sharing any of the presuppositions of the chief actors in the scene. The centurion will have meant 'son of God' in a pagan sense, no doubt the sense of Roman religion, 'a noble, revered, holy, heroic person, worthy of the gods'. To Christians and to the evangelists they were saying more than they knew. The gospel undoubtedly understands their confession in the Christian sense.

vv.55-56 The chosen Twelve had all fled, but the faithful women are there, 'looking on from a distance'. This is a fulfilment of Psalm 38:11: 'My friends and companions stand aloof from my affliction'. It is no coincidence that the same women witness Jesus' death, his burial and the empty tomb (*Matthew* 27:61 and 28:1). Their testimony stands firm.

No one, not even the holiest person, was ever able to take on the sins of all people and make an offering as a sacrifice for all. The existence in Christ of the divine person of the Son, who at once surpasses and embraces all human persons, and constitutes himself as the head of all humanity, makes possible his redemptive sacrifice for all.

(Catechism of the Catholic Church n. 616)

The Burial of Jesus

vv.57-60 Legends have grown up around Joseph of Arimathea. The gospel gives us only fascinating hints. 'Arimathea' is the Aramaic name for the coastal town Ramathaim, presumably his birth-place. Mark tells us that he was awaiting the kingdom of God (*Mark* 15:43), which Matthew understands as (literally) 'he had been discipled to Jesus'. More intriguing, Mark also tells us that he was 'a respected member of the council'.

The bodies of criminals were not allowed to be taken by the members of their families, but were buried in a common grave. Was Joseph the council-member charged with this, and was 'his new tomb' not his personally but as the counsellor charged with criminal burials? The fact that it was new is not merely a matter of respect for Jesus, as was the clean shroud. A normal rock-cut tomb-chamber has about six low two metre long shafts leading off it, for the repose of six bodies. If there had been other bodies in Jesus' tomb-chamber there would have been room for dispute about the identity of the missing body. This was not possible in the case of a hitherto unused tomb.

There was a whole hillside of tombs just outside the city, only a few metres from the traditional site of Golgotha, on the edge of the same quarry. The design of a rock-tomb in the Holy Land is standard: from ground level a few stone steps lead down to a short passage. Then comes the closure, a great millstone, rolled across in a groove. Inside is a tomb-chamber, an empty space, two metres by two metres by two metres. On each of the three sides (not the side of entry) are two narrow shafts for bodies. These can all be re-used, for when the flesh has corrupted the bones are placed in a casket and removed.

Tomb with rolling stone.

The Guard at the Tomb

vv.62-66 This little scene between Pilate and the Jewish leaders occurs only in Matthew, confirming yet again the determination to stamp out the Jesus movement. It is interesting that the Pharisees here reappear, having taken no part in the trial and death of Jesus. Perhaps their characteristic caution (the less you do, the fewer rules you break!) had prevented them taking definite action. Perhaps their objections were to Jesus' teaching rather than his person. Pilate holds aloof, with a tinge of sarcasm, suggesting that they ought to know their own business, with perhaps even an implied challenge about preventing the predicted resurrection.

Ivory diptych from Milan Cathedral.

The Word Lives on

As already pointed out, the whole of Matthew's Passion Narrative is read on Palm Sunday in Year A.

When Johann Sebastian Bach put to music in his 'St Matthew Passion' the section about the centurion, the words of approval of Jesus, which are spoken by the 'the centurion and those with him', are given to the Chorus, and not to one individual soloist. In this way he expresses beautifully the cosmic nature of this profession of faith.

St Longinus the centurion in St Peter's Basilica in Rome.

Live the Word of God

What do you hear now?

Suggestions for reflection and prayer

Read Psalm 22 and pray it with Jesus on the cross

- Pray for those who are driven to despair by suffering, that they may see God's love.
- Pray for all those who suffer and die by violence, that they may receive God's strength and forgive their persecutors.
- Pray for those who inflict violence, that they may receive a change of heart.

Reflect on the obedience of Jesus to the Father throughout his life, and especially at the consummate moment of crucifixion.

- Pray to be able to participate in this obedience, as an adopted child of God, with Jesus.
- Pray for those who feel abandoned by God, that they may know his forgiveness.

Reflect on the joy of being drawn from the tomb by Jesus into his heavenly company.

- Pray for all the dead, that they may know the joy of the resurrection.
- Pray for the dead who are especially dear to you.

The state of the dead Christ is the mystery of the tomb and the descent into hell. It is the mystery of Holy Saturday, when Christ, lying in the tomb, reveals God's great Sabbath rest after the fulfilment of salvation, which brings peace to the whole universe.

(Catechism of the Catholic Church n. 624)

The Empty Tomb and Resurrection Meetings

Hear the Word of God

Read: Matthew 28:1-20

28:1 After the sabbath, as the first day of the week was dawning, Mary Magdalene and the other Mary went to see the tomb. 2 And suddenly there was a great earthquake; for an angel of the Lord, descending from heaven, came and rolled back the stone and sat on it. 3 His appearance was like lightning, and his clothing white as snow. 4 For fear of him the guards shook and became like dead men. 5 But the angel said to the women, 'Do not be afraid; I know that you are looking for Jesus who was crucified. 6 He is not here; for he has been raised, as he said. Come, see the place where he lay. 7 Then go quickly and tell his disciples, 'He has been raised from the dead, and indeed he is going ahead of you to Galilee; there you will see him.' This is my message for you.' 8 So they left the tomb quickly with fear and great joy, and ran to tell his disciples. 9 Suddenly Jesus met them and said, 'Greetings!' And they came to him, took hold of his feet, and worshipped him. 10 Then Jesus said to them, 'Do not be afraid; go and tell my brothers to go to Galilee; there they will see me.'

11 While they were going, some of the guard went into the city and told the chief priests everything that had happened. 12 After the priests had assembled with the elders, they devised a plan to give a large sum of money to the soldiers, 13 telling them, 'You must say, 'His disciples came by night and stole him away while we were asleep.' 14 If this comes to the governor's ears, we will satisfy him and keep you out of trouble.' 15 So they took the money and did as they were directed. And this story is still told among the Jews to this day.

16 Now the eleven disciples went to Galilee, to the mountain to which Jesus had directed them. 17 When they saw him, they worshipped him; but some doubted. 18 And Jesus came and said to them, 'All authority in heaven and on earth has been given to me. 19 Go therefore and make disciples of all nations, baptizing them in the name of the Father and of the Son and of the Holy Spirit, 20 and teaching them to obey everything that I have commanded you. And remember, I am with you always, to the end of the age.'

Opposite: The Marys at the Tomb by Duccio di Buoninsegna.

Understand the Word of God

This session will explore:

- ❖ the stories of the meetings with the Risen Christ
- ❖ the risen Christ and the risen Christian
- ❖ Matthew's tussle with Judaism
- ❖ the mission to the world

Setting in the Gospel

The narrative of the empty tomb is in many ways the climax of the gospel. Without it the gospel would make no sense. It is not, of course, the narrative of the resurrection, for that could never be described. Is the resurrection even correctly described as an event within history? It is the juncture of time and eternity, for it is the transition of the dead Jesus into the living state of glory.

Perhaps even more important the resurrection is the intervention of God in the world to vindicate his son Jesus Christ after his consummate act of love and obedience. God takes him 'to his side', 'to enthrone him in heaven'. There is no way of avoiding the inadequate human language and imagery. The Risen Christ is the first-fruits of the new world, to be followed by all those who are in Christ. One might say that the resurrection starts in history, because it took place at a certain time and place, with a 'before' and an 'after', but ends outside history, since there is no time or place in heaven.

The story of the empty tomb as told by Mark concentrated on the awe, shock, terror and fright of the women (*Mark* 16:8). They do not inspect the tomb but run away terrified, delaying only to hear the angel's explanation. The gospel does not spell out the reason for their terror, but we may see it as the reaction to the divine intervention.

It was commonly accepted by the Jews, with the exception of the Sadducees, that at the end of time the general resurrection of the dead would take place. There was no concept of a single person rising alone. The witness of the angel shows that this final intervention of

God is beginning to occur. As from an earthquake, tidal wave, volcanic eruption or tsunami, the natural reaction is to flee, to get away from the spot.

To the narrative of the empty tomb in Mark 16:1-8, Matthew adds another apocalyptic symbol in the form of an earthquake (verse 2). He turns the terrified women into the first messengers of the good news (verse 8). There follow three other incidents: a meeting with the Risen Christ (verses 9-10), the silencing of the sentries (verses 11-15) and a final commission to the eleven disciples (verses 16-20).

The Resurrection by Piero della Francesca.

What kind of text?

These four stories are of very different types of material. The story of the empty tomb is a studious attempt to avoid attempting to describe the indescribable. The chief actor or subject, the Risen Christ, is not there, and the human witnesses have to be content with reporting the earthquake and the angel's message.

The second incident, the meeting of Christ with the women, is the first of several meetings recorded in various overlapping traditions. Paul refers to meetings with the Risen Christ which are not included in the four gospels, but which were passed on and learnt by heart as the basic material of faith (1 *Corinthians* 15:3-5).

The bribing of the sentries is designed to scotch any report that Jesus had indeed risen. The commission on the mountain in Galilee can also be seen as the climax of the gospel, setting the scene for the whole evangelistic effort of the Church.

Following the great English scholar C.H. Dodd, these meetings are commonly classified in two groups. Meetings such as the one with the women prove the reality of the Resurrection. In other meetings a commission is given to the disciples, as in the final verses of this chapter.

Sunrise

Commentary: verse by verse reading

The Empty Tomb

v.1 There is no slavish attempt to reduce the stories of the empty tomb to uniformity. One wonders even whether Matthew deliberately intended to correct Mark. He cuts out Salome and reduces 'Mary the mother of James' in Mark 16:1 to merely 'the other Mary'. More importantly, Jew that he is, he changes their reason for coming. Instead of coming to anoint Jesus they come to fulfil the pious Jewish custom of visiting the tombs of the beloved. This seems more reasonable than the dubious process of anointing a body after three days in the tomb in the heat of the Holy Land. Furthermore, no Palestinian tomb-closer that I have ever seen could be moved by three people, let alone three women.

vv.2-3 Just as he did at the death of Jesus (27:51), Matthew shows the 'earth-shaking' nature of this moment by introducing an earthquake into the story. This is part of the apocalyptic style of writing which was common in Judaism at this time. Matthew is also more explicit about the heavenly messenger. While Mark simply shows from the description of his clothing that the young man is a heavenly being, Matthew says outright that he is the angel of the Lord, well-known to his Jewish audience as the Old Testament go-between to bring God's purposes into the world.

v.4 The guards, not mentioned at all by Mark, are introduced to prepare the reader for their sinister part in the next incident of the story.

vv.5-6 As in many passages of the Old Testament, the function of the *angelus interpres*, or interpreting angel, is to explain the significance of an event or dream or vision, giving the divine meaning of a coded vision or a puzzling happening. The disciples would not have needed much urging to return to Galilee, their homeland, after their hopes had been shattered by the ignominious death of their Master, despite this new turn of events.

The interpreting angel speaks to the visionary in Revelation 22:6:

'These words are trustworthy and true, for the Lord, the God of the spirits of the prophets, has sent his angel to show his servants what must soon take place.'

In this gospel the angel's message, unlike that in Mark 16:7, includes no explicit mention of telling Peter, so that the last we see of the leader of the apostles is when he is 'weeping bitterly' after denying any knowledge of Jesus (26:75). In other ways Matthew pays special attention to Peter in the gospel. Perhaps he does not want to appear to soften Peter's guilt here by the implication of Jesus' forgiveness.

v.8 By contrast to Mark's account, the women, far from being silenced by terror, are overjoyed and accept the commission to pass on the good news. This is perhaps Matthew's female equivalent to the charge given to the male disciples in the final verses of the gospel.

Jesus Meets the Women

vv.9-10 This little incident seems to duplicate or even trump the previous scene. If Jesus gives the message personally, the angel becomes somewhat superfluous. John 20:14-18 has a similar scene between the Risen Jesus and Mary Magdalene, also a touching and affectionate meeting. It is, however, of the nature of oral tradition that the details of a story differ in each telling.

The Three Marys at the Sepulchre, c.1800 by William Blake, (1757-1827).

The Guards are Bribed

vv.11-15 As many authors have pointed out from ancient times, the story concocted by the chief priests is pretty weak! If the guards had been asleep they would not have seen the body-snatchers, still less been able to identify them as disciples of Jesus. The story, and indeed, the whole mention of guards at the tomb, comes only in Matthew. It may be a product of the hostility between Matthew's community of Christians sprung from Judaism and their fellow-religionists who did not accept Jesus as Messiah.

The removal of the stone blocking the entrance to a tomb would have been such a major operation that sentries were scarcely necessary to guard the sealed tomb.

The Final Commission

v.16 We do not know where in Galilee this scene took place, since Matthew simply says 'on the mountain'. Jesus takes his place authoritatively, just as Moses had done, and as he himself had done for the Sermon on the Mount.

v.17 The trait of failing to recognise Jesus recurs in most of the meetings with the Risen Lord: the disciples on the road to Emmaus (*Luke*), Mary Magdalene in the garden (*John*), the disciples in the upper room (*Luke*), the disciples on the Lake of Galilee (*John* 21). Jesus seems to have been somehow transformed in appearance. We can know little about the risen body. Certainly it was not subject to the familiar limitations of time and space, for the Risen Lord could enter closed spaces.

Paul says that to ask how the risen body will be is a silly question. He goes on to explain three changes: what was corruptible becomes incorruptible, what was contemptible becomes glorious, what was weak becomes strong (1 *Corinthians* 15:42-44). All these changes bring the risen person into the sphere of the divine.

Acts 11:26 maintains that it was at Antioch that the disciples were first called 'Christians'. There was a large and prosperous Jewish colony in that city. The disciples of Jesus were called 'Christians', a name rather mocking in form, or 'Messianists' because they recognised a Messiah, namely Jesus. The fall of Jerusalem in 70 AD led to mockery and persecution of the Jews of Antioch by the Greeks. If Matthew was written at Antioch – which is a good possibility, though by no means certain - his community was a persecuted minority of a persecuted minority, not a pleasant position to be in!

Luke 24:15-16 While they were talking and discussing, Jesus himself came near and went with them, but their eyes were kept from recognising him.

John 20:14 When she had said this, she turned around and saw Jesus standing there, but she did not know that it was Jesus.

Luke 24:37 They were startled and terrified, and thought that they were seeing a ghost.

John 21:4 Just after daybreak, Jesus stood on the beach, but the disciples did not know that it was Jesus.

If Christ has not been raised, your faith is futile and you are still in your sins. How are the dead raised? With what kind of body do they come? Fool! What you sow does not come to life unless it dies. So it is with the resurrection of the dead.

(1 Corinthians 15:17, 35-36, 42)

Daniel 7:13-14

I saw one like a son of man coming with the clouds of heaven.

And he came to the Ancient One and was presented before him.

To him was given dominion and glory and kingship.

Arise, shine, for your light has come and the glory of the Lord has risen upon you. Nations shall come to your light and kings to the brightness of your dawn.

(Isaiah 60:1,3)

On that day living waters shall flow out from Jerusalem. It shall continue in summer as in winter. Then all who survive of the nations shall go up year by year to worship the King, the Lord of hosts, and to keep the festival of booths.

(Zechariah 14:8,16)

Paul is of course teaching about the risen and transformed Christian, but the basis of all his teaching is that the Risen Christ is the new Adam, the model and template for the risen Christian. About changed appearance he says nothing. Is it possible that the joy and happiness consequent on the raising to the divine of the human nature of Jesus were so transforming that he was not immediately recognisable even to his friends?

v.18 The Risen Christ prefaces his commission to the Eleven with his right to authority by reference to Daniel's vision of the Son of Man (*Daniel* 7:13-14). To the Son of Man in that vision was given all authority on earth. To the Risen Christ has been given all authority in heaven and on earth.

Authority on earth and in heaven was given first to Peter (16:19), then to the Church (18:18). Christ's statement now explains why the Church (and Peter) have such authority. It is channelled through him, for, as he says in the last verse of all, he himself is present in the Church, supporting it always. This has been a persistent emphasis of Matthew's gospel, from Jesus' angelic naming 'Emmanuel' (1:23) onwards. Matthew 1:23 and 28:20, with their major emphasis on the presence of Christ, bracket the gospel.

vv.19-20 Despite Matthew's Jewish pedigree he does not hesitate to report the extension of the mission to all the world, Gentiles included. To burst the bounds of Judaism was a unique emphasis of Jesus. After the return from Babylon Judaism became increasingly aware of its salvific mission to the whole world, but it was couched in terms of the world coming to draw salvation from Jerusalem.

Now the movement is in the other direction: disciples of Jesus are to go out to the world. Such was also the direction and perception of Paul: it was no longer necessary to observe the Jewish Law in order to obtain the fulfilment of the promises made to Abraham. The breakthrough comes in Jesus' acceptance of the Syro-Phoenician woman whose daughter he accepts to cure (*Mark* 7:24-30), or in Jesus' rejection of the food laws of Judaism (*Mark* 7:18-23). Then Paul insists that salvation and the gift of the Spirit come through putting all our hope in Christ, not through observing the Jewish Law (*Galatians* 3:1-3).

The formula to be used for baptism is fascinating. It is the most explicit statement of the three Persons of the Trinity in the New Testament, a teaching which is frequently hinted in many ways in the New Testament, but which remains to be made explicit.

In the Acts of the Apostles it is clear that baptism was 'into the name of Jesus' (Acts 8:16). Those baptised put themselves under his protection (for the name signifies the power or protection). Then the followers of Jesus are described as those over whom the name of Jesus has been invoked.

On the other hand, baptism is also somehow incomplete without the descent of the Spirit. So Peter and John go down to Samaria to impart the Spirit to the newly baptised (Acts 8:16). When Peter is about to baptise Cornelius and his household the Spirit nips in beforehand (Acts 10:44). When Paul finds at Ephesus disciples who have been baptised only with John's baptism, he lays his hands on them and 'the Holy Spirit came upon them' (Acts 19:6).

Paul VI was the first pope to visit the United Nations in New York on 4th October 1965.

The Word Lives on

Parts of this joyful chapter are read quite frequently at the Eucharist. Matthew's version of the empty tomb story forms the gospel reading for the Easter Vigil in Year A. The story of the meeting with the women is read on Easter Monday. The final commission forms the gospel for the Solemnity of the Ascension in Year A. It is used also for the Solemnity of the Holy Trinity in Year B because of the unique trinitarian formula.

On the feast of the Japanese martyrs (Paul Miki and others) Matthew 28:16-20 reminds us of the far-flung spread of the gospel. It is recommended for feasts of pastors as an inspiration for mission.

Resurrection Icon by Sophie Hacker, Cotgrave Church, Nottinghamshire, UK.

Live the Word of God

Listen again to the reading: Matthew 28:1-20

What do you hear now?
Suggestions for reflection and prayer

Reflect on Jesus' resurrection as the model of ours. What would this transformation into the sphere of the divine mean? How would I be changed?

- ❖ Pray for a deeper understanding of the end of life, and a firmer confidence in the loving welcome of God.
- ❖ Pray for all the faithful departed, that they may come into the happiness of the company of the Lord.

Reflect on what it would be like actually to meet the Risen Lord? What would your reaction be if you were Mary Magdalene or the other Mary? Joy or unworthiness or both?

- ❖ Pray for the single-mindedness to come to know the Risen Lord.
- ❖ Pray for the purity to be able to greet the Lord, even hesitantly.
- ❖ Pray for the complete purity of relaxing in the embrace of the Most High.

Reflect on the mission of the Church, its needs, its diversity, its implications for human solidarity. What can I do to help?

- ❖ Pray for the needs of the Church and of those who are still beyond the reach of the Church.
- ❖ Pray for a greater understanding of the mystery of the Holy Trinity and the part which the three Persons must play in our life.
- ❖ Pray for the wisdom to see and the courage to do your part in bringing Christ to those who have not heard the gospel.

From 'The Gift of Scripture', a document of the Bishops of England and Wales, and of Scotland:

The Gospel of Matthew, which had begun with the magi from distant lands, ends with the mission to the nations. Jesus, who came first for his own Jewish people, sends out the disciples to teach the gospel to all nations and to baptise. (n.52)

Picture Credits

Cover   Lindisfarne Gospels, St Matthew, c700. British Library, London, Great Britain. ©Photo Scala Florence/HIP

P.9   The Magi and King Herod, from Bellver de Cerdanya, 14th cent. , Catalan art. Episcopal Museum, Vich, Spain. ©Photo Scala, Florence

P.11   ©Photos.com

P.12   ©Photos.com

P.13   Massacre of the Innocents, 1565, Pieter the Elder Bruegel, (1528-1569) Kunsthistorisches Museum, Vienna, Austria. ©Photo Austrian Archive/Scala Florence

P.16   The Flight into Egypt. ©JesusMafa.com

P.19   Ms Lat Q.v.I.126 f.36 The Massacre of the Innocents, from the 'Book of Hours of Louis d'Orleans', 1469, Colombe, Jean (c.1430-c.93) / National Library, St. Petersburg, Russia / The Bridgeman Art Library

P.20   The entrance to Nativity Church in Bethlehem. ©BiblePlaces.com

P.22   The Sermon on the Mount , Fra Angelico, (1387-1455). Museo di San Marco, Florence, Italy. ©Photo Scala, Florence - courtesy of the Ministero Beni e Att. Culturali

P.25   Mount of Beatitudes hillside in spring. ©BiblePlaces.com

P.29   ©Stock.Xchng

P.31   The Sermon on the Mount, from the Sistine Chapel, c.1481-83), Cosimo Rosselli, (1439-1507) / Vatican Museums and Galleries, Vatican City, Italy / The Bridgeman Art Library

P.32   Church of the Beatitudes. ©Photos.com

P.34   Jesus Calms the Storm, 1995, Laura James, (Contemporary Artist) / Private Collection / The Bridgeman Art Library

P.37   After the Miracle of the Evil Spirits Turned into Swine, Italian School, (15th century) / Biblioteca Reale, Turin, Italy / Alinari / The Bridgeman Art Library

P.41   The Two Men Possessed with Unclean Spirits, illustration for 'The Life of Christ', c.1884-96, James Jacques Joseph Tissot, (1836-1902) / Brooklyn Museum of Art, New York, USA / Purchased by Public Subscription / The Bridgeman Art Library

P.43   Icon depicting the Healing of the Paralytic, 1811, Bulgarian School, (19th century) / Rila Monastery National Museum, Bulgaria / Archives Charmet / The Bridgeman Art Library

P.44   Jesus heals the paralysed Man. ©JesusMafa.com

P.46   Plaque depicting Christ blessing the Apostles, Constantinople, Byzantine, (10th century) / Louvre, Paris, France / The Bridgeman Art Library

P.49   ©Photos.com

P.50   ©Photos.com